Praise for

WHY WE KISS UNDER THE MISTLETOE

"This marvelous book may present itself as a Silver Stream on the open road, but under the hood it is a heavy-duty all-wheel pick-up with tremendous historical grit. Michael Foley has neatly balanced the popular style of the book with careful research in biblical (and especially) historical insight. In a word, it "works," and well. The book is lively and engaging and teeming with a historian's experience and familiarity with a vast array of intriguing subjects. Highly recommended."

> —**STEVEN C. SMITH**, author of *The House of the Lord*

"Why We Kiss nder the Mistletoe does more than tell us about the clever ways we've justified our stolen smooches. It ranges across cultures and languages, history and lore, poetry and song, and then it takes this one life we have and the forms and trappings of one of its most joyous expressions and puts them all under the revelatory power of a Drummond light—all without making us feel as if we're reading a master's thesis on the etiology of the aetosaur's eating habits or some other topic of inexpressible tedium."

> —**JASON PETERS**, professor of English, Hillsdale College

WHY WE KISS UNDER THE MISTLETOE

WHY WE *Kiss*
UNDER THE
Mistletoe

CHRISTMAS TRADITIONS
EXPLAINED

MICHAEL P. FOLEY
AUTHOR OF 'DRINKING WITH THE SAINTS'

REGNERY
HISTORY
Washington, D.C.

Regnery History™ is a trademark of Salem Communications Holding Corporation
Regnery® is a registered trademark and its colophon is a trademark of Salem Communications Holding Corporation

ISBN: 978-1-68451-241-6
eISBN: 978-1-68451-281-2

Published in the United States by
Regnery History
An Imprint of Regnery Publishing
A Division of Salem Media Group
Washington, D.C.
www.RegneryHistory.com

Manufactured in the United States of America

10 9 8 7 6 5 4 3 2 1

Books are available in quantity for promotional or premium use. For information on discounts and terms, please visit our website: www.Regnery.com.

To the master of holiday books, the Reverend Francis X. Weiser, S.J., and to all the members, living and deceased, of the "Christmas Parish" of which he was pastor, Holy Trinity German Catholic Church in Boston, Massachusetts

Contents

INTRODUCTION

*In all the civilized world there is no spot so secluded,
and, perhaps, no heart so dark that the sound of
Christmas chimes fails to awaken in it a sense of joy
and exultation. Round and round the earth rolls the
grand sympathetic melody, calling on rich and poor
alike, to put aside for a day all disputes and jealou-
sies; and over and above all trouble and perplexity
swells the sublime, reiterated strain: "Peace and
good-will, good-will and peace, peace and good-will
to all mankind."*[1]

The anonymous author who wrote these words in 1871 may have been a bit melodramatic, but his claim still strikes a chord today. What is it about Christmas that continues to captivate our hearts? Is it the childhood memories of presents under the tree? The sentimental music? The sense of coziness? Certainly the religious reason, the birth of the Savior, is cause for celebration, but most people hold Christmas dearer to their hearts than Easter, which is technically the more important feast in the Christian year. Why Christmas?

This book helps to answer that question by giving you a history of the holiday and the meaning behind the customs that make it so special. In this book you will learn just about everything you need to know not only about the big day itself but about the long buildup to it and the comet tail of celebrations following it. While most Christmas books cover only a few days of the year, we will take you through over two months of merriment—and cover customs treasured in dozens of different cultures, spanning twenty centuries of history.

One of many Norman Rockwell Christmas-issue magazine covers. *American Boy*

And as we do, we will carefully separate fact from fiction, unearthing the true meaning behind many of our most beloved Christmas customs and tales. The Christmas story is so storied that there are now even myths about Christmas myths. With an impartial but loving eye, we lay out the various theories about why we do what we do. Where does the Santa Claus legend really come from? Is the Christmas tree a pagan yuletide observance? What exactly is a carol? Is Groundhog Day a part of the Christmas cycle? And, of course, why do we kiss under the mistletoe?

Finally, we introduce you to a side of Christmas that you did not know existed, from forgotten traditions of mischief and mayhem to ghoulish figures haunting the holiest of nights.

All told, this book will introduce you to hundreds of magical figures, foods, drinks, songs, superstitions, practices, and, above all, stories about the most wonderful time of the year.

It is our hope that this book will deepen your appreciation of the Christmas season and enable you to celebrate it with heightened understanding and greater joy.

Merry Christmas!

Chapter One

CHRISTMAS'S ROLLER COASTER PAST

The origins of Christmas are more tangled than an old box of Christmas lights, and its history is rowdier than a 1960s holiday office party.

ORIGINS

Let's start with the origins. The Gospels according to Matthew and Luke provide the only canonical accounts that we have of the birth of Jesus Christ. According to these narratives, the Blessed Virgin Mary and St. Joseph were "espoused," that is, they had completed the first stage of a first-century Jewish wedding (the signing of the marriage contract) but not the second (the introduction of the bride to her husband's home, which could be months and sometimes more than a year later). During that waiting period, Mary conceived the Christ Child through the agency of the Holy Spirit and then left town for three months to help her aged cousin St. Elizabeth give birth to St. John the Baptist. When she returned, St. Joseph noticed that she was with child. After being told by an angel in a dream to take Mary to wife (that is, to complete the second stage of the wedding, taking her into his home) and to adopt Jesus as his own, he did so.[1] As the time drew near for Mary to bear her Son, the holy couple traveled from their home in Nazareth to Bethlehem in order to be enrolled in a Roman census. Because there was no room for them in an inn, Mary delivered her Child in a stable, which according to oral tradition was a sheltered cave (where Bethlehem's Basilica of the Nativity now stands). Angels announced the good news to nearby shepherds, who came to adore Him, and Magi who had been following a star from the East did so as well, but only after they had paid a visit to King Herod to inquire into the whereabouts of the newborn King. The question unsettled the paranoid and wicked Herod, who ordered the death of all baby boys in Bethlehem in an attempt to eliminate the competition. Joseph, however, was warned of Herod's plot in a dream and fled with the Holy Family to Egypt. After Herod died, another dream told Joseph that it was safe to return to Nazareth.

Critics of the infancy narratives claim that the facts do not add up: Herod the Great was not king when the census of Quirinius was taken but rather died four years before the birth of Christ; the census would not have been taken during the winter and would not have required bringing one's expectant wife; there were no astronomical anomalies (no "Christmas star") that we know of in 1 B.C.–A.D. 1, and so forth. Biblical critics also claim that because the story of Jesus' birth resembles that of Moses in some respects (both, for example, involve the slaughter of innocent boys), it must be fictitious.[2]

There are, however, compelling points in favor of the original Christmas story. The Christmas star need not have been an astronomical event; it could have been a miraculous apparition limited to the Magi. We should not be hasty in drawing conclusions about dating: it is difficult to align three different ancient calendars (the Jewish lunar calendar, the Roman solar calendar, and a different Greek solar calendar). The conclusion that Herod died in 4 B.C. (four years before the birth of Christ) is based on a miscalculation of a passage in the writings of Flavius Josephus. And if you posit that the Magi met the Holy Family after their return to Nazareth rather than, as is popularly imagined, in the stable at Bethlehem, the chronology lines up.[3] As for the belief that the story of Christ's birth must be false because it resembles Moses's, there is no logical necessity to think so. The resemblance could be coincidental or, better yet, part of God's master plan, in which case the parallels are proof of the story's veracity rather than its falsity.[4]

DATES

As for when we observe Jesus Christ's birthday, we know that in the late second or early third century Christians in Egypt celebrated Christ's birth *and* His baptism as an adult in the River Jordan on January 6 and that other Eastern-rite Christians eventually followed suit. In Rome, on the other hand, there is evidence that Christmas was celebrated on December 25 as early as A.D. 336. Eventually (from the fourth century on), the East adopted December 25 as the date of Christ's birth and January 6 as the date of His baptism while the West kept its Christmas date of December 25 and adopted January 6 as the visit of the Magi (though it also commemorated Christ's baptism on January 6). To this day, there is a difference in emphasis between the calendars of Western Christians (Roman Catholics and Protestants) and Eastern Christians (Eastern Orthodox, Oriental Orthodox, Church of the East, and Eastern-Rite Catholics). In the West, there is a buildup to Christmas as the big day and then a plateauing that lasts until the lesser Feast of the Epiphany on January 6. In the East, Christmas Day is important, but "Theophany" (January 6) is the grand high point of the season; indeed, it is second only to Easter in the entire year.

How these dates were chosen remains a hotly debated topic. There are three main theories.

The first, the "history of religion" theory, is that Christians in Rome chose December 25 to supplant a Roman pagan festival called the Birth of the Unconquered Sun and that Christians in Egypt chose January 6 to supplant an Egyptian festival of the god Aion, who was born of a virgin.[5] Although this theory has enjoyed the most scholarly support over the years, it has been criticized for overlooking one important detail. Christmas may not have been celebrated on December 25 until 336, but Christians were nonetheless talking about December 25 as the date of Jesus' birthday as early as 240. The Roman feast of the Unconquered Sun, on the other hand, was not instituted until 274. Did Christians try to coopt a pagan feast, or did pagans try to coopt a Christian date? Most likely neither. The Roman Emperor Aurelian, who instituted the celebration of the Unconquered Sun, was more concerned about the winter solstice (which at the time fell on December 25) than about stealing thunder from a small religious minority.[6] Either way, Christians were not thinking of pagan customs when they first arrived at a date for their Savior's birth.

Which brings us to the second hypothesis, called the "calculation" theory. According to this view, early Christians were influenced by the Jewish notion of an "integral age," the belief that the prophets died on the same date as their birth. Some early Christians calculated that April

6 was the date of Christ's crucifixion, while others thought that it was March 25. March 25 became the date of Christ's *conception* in the womb (the Feast of the Annunciation), and nine months after March 25 is December 25. Similarly, if you add nine months to April 6, you get January 6.[7] The theory is intriguing, but unfortunately there is no evidence that the early Church knew about the rabbinical belief in an integral age, nor does the theory explain why Christians would have modified the belief from a two-pronged focus on birth and death to the three prongs of conception, birth, and death.[8]

Finally, there is the third theory, which is that Jesus Christ was actually born on or around December 25.[9] King David had divided the Levitical priesthood into twenty-four "courses" (1 Chronicles 24:7–18), and the Gospel according to St. Luke records that Zechariah, who was burning incense in the Temple when he had a vision of St. Gabriel the Archangel, was in the course of Abijah (Luke 1:5). Calculating from Luke's account and Talmudic sources, we can conclude that Zechariah's turn to serve in the Temple as a member of his course most likely happened during the week of September 5–11 in the year before Jesus' birth. Assuming that John the Baptist was conceived shortly thereafter (Luke 1:23–24), he would have been born somewhere between June 20 and 26. Jesus was six months' younger than His cousin (Luke 1:36), so He would have been born between December 21 and 27. This thesis, however, has yet to gain widespread acceptance.

So who is right? Here's what we know:

In former ages and even in some places today, birth-dates were not of great concern—either because the actual date of birth was difficult to determine or because there were other, more important factors to take into consideration. In ancient Greece, Plato's birthday was celebrated on the Feast of Apollo: either the great phi-losopher forgot to tell his disciples when his birthday was, or his disciples thought it more important to associ-ate him with the god of light, beauty, and poetry. In some Christian cultures even today, one's name day (the feast day of the saint after whom one is named) is a bigger celebration than one's birthday. In Japan, where the group is traditionally more important than the individ-ual, there were no personal birthday celebrations prior to the influence of American culture in the 1950s. The old Japanese equivalent of a birthday was either New Year's Day (when everyone knew he was a year older) or Girls' Day on March 3 (for all daughters and mothers) and Boys' Day on May 5 (for all sons and fathers).

Second, even in the unlikely event that the early Chris-tians decided to celebrate the birth of Christ on Decem-ber 25 to coopt a pagan holiday, they clearly understood the difference between their religion and the one they were supplanting. Church leaders sternly rebuked con-verts who retained even the external symbols of the old festivals, as the writings of Tertullian, St. Augustine, and Pope St. Leo the Great attest. And the doctrine of the

Incarnation, which teaches that Jesus Christ is 100 percent human and 100 percent divine, is not the same as stories of demigods being 50 percent human and 50 percent divine. Understanding the pedigree of demigods requires no more imagination than following a family tree chart on ancestry.com, whereas understanding how the Divine Person Jesus Christ is not only the Son of Man but also consubstantial with the Father demands a whole new metaphysical skill set. As the Christian believer sees it, there is not so much a *pagan* yearning for the gods that Christianity replaced as there is a *human* yearning for the divine that paganism responded to imperfectly and tragically, and that Christianity purifies and fulfills joyfully.

Third, say what you will, the symbolism works. The Bible describes Jesus Christ as the Light or the Sun or the Dawn, and so it is appropriate that His birthday is celebrated around the time of the winter solstice. A Jewish boy is circumcised eight days after his birth, and so if Jesus' birthday is celebrated on December 25, it is appropriate to commemorate His circumcision on January 1 (Luke 2:21). In accordance with the Mosaic Law, Jesus was presented in the Temple and His mother was ritually purified forty days after His birth (Luke 2:22–24), and so it is appropriate to celebrate this event on February 2, the Feast of the Purification of the Blessed Virgin Mary (a.k.a. the Feast of the Presentation of the Lord). The Bible states that John the Baptist is six months older than the Messiah (Luke 1:24–26), and so it is appropriate that his birthday is said to fall six months later (June 24). St. John the Baptist famously says of Jesus, "He must increase, but I must decrease" (John 3:30), and so it is appropriate that John's birthday be celebrated on or after the summer solstice, when the days start to grow longer. The Blessed Virgin Mary conceived by the Holy Spirit nine months before giving birth to Jesus, and so it is appropriate that the Feast of the Annunciation is celebrated on March 25, a date that follows the spring equinox and marks the end of the dead, dark winter and the beginning of a new era of life and rebirth.

And for those who enjoy straining their brains, these dates afford matter for deeper, more mystical explorations. St. Augustine notes that there are 276 days between March 25 and December 25, which happens to be the sum of 46 x 6. Forty-six is the number of years that it took to build the Holy Temple (John 2:20), and six (for reasons too complicated to explain here) is the symbol for one year. Thus 276 is an apt numerical symbol of the Temple that is Christ's own body (John 2:21), which was built up from a single zygote on March 25 to a newborn baby on December 25.[10] Mind blown? Merry Christmas!

MEDIEVAL MERRIMENT AND MISCHIEF

Christmas got off to a slow start in comparison to Easter and even some saints' feast days, but it more than caught up. As a sign of its new importance, Christmas marked the beginning of the new Church year from the fifth to the tenth century (curiously, the Inuit in the Arctic circle still begin the new year on Christmas the same). In A.D. 425 the Roman emperor banned chariot races, which were popular but cruel, on Christmas Day, and a century later the emperor declared Christmas a civic holiday during which work and public business were prohibited. In 506, the Council of Agde urged Christians to receive Holy Communion on Christmas Day, in 563 the Council of Braga forbade fasting on Christmas, and in 567 the Council of Tours established the Twelve Days of Christmas from December 25 to January 6 and mandated fasting during Advent to prepare for the great feast. Christmas also became the occasion for important events. In the year 496 St. Remigius baptized King Clovis I and three thousand Franks, in 598 St. Augustine of Canterbury baptized ten thousand Britons, and in 800 the Pope crowned Charlemagne head of the new Holy Roman Empire, all on Christmas Day. The holy day was on its way.

Christmas was enormously popular during the Middle Ages, and it is thanks to our medieval forebears that we have many of our familiar Christmas customs, such as caroling, Yule logs, Nativity scenes, Christmas pageants, and so on (see Chapters Eight through Eleven). But the holiday was not quite the same then as it is now. As we will see in Chapter Twelve, Christmastime was a season of misrule. Customs such as the Feast of Fools and the Boy Bishop upended the social hierarchy that prevailed during the rest of the year and relieved folks of the roles they usually played in their daily lives. Christmas also had a dark side (the subject of Chapter Seven), confronting primal fears about winter and pagan superstitions about the season. Christmas in the Middle Ages was less a private celebration of family and children and more a public occasion for adult feasting and tippling—and as we will see in Chapter Ten, some of these delights are still with us.

On the other hand, despite their vices, medieval Christians understood the religious core of the holiday and cherished it. It was not unusual for the faithful to attend three Masses on Christmas Day (one at midnight, one at dawn, and one later in the morning) and to participate in religious services throughout the Twelve Days of Christmas. And with the love of God came a love of neighbor. Many medieval Christmas customs involved extra solicitude for the poor and kindness to all. Even the animals benefited from this seasonal largesse as they were spared from labor and feasted on extra hay.

THE WORLD TURNED UPSIDE DOWN

The raucous medieval Christmas was asking for a backlash, and a backlash it got. For centuries the Catholic clergy tried to stem or outlaw abuses while keeping the spirit of the holiday, with varying degrees of success. But the first total assault on Christmas, by people who were willing to throw the baby out with the bath water, took place during the Protestant Reformation. Martin Luther was fine with the holiday, but other Reformers, such as Ulrich Zwingli, and later Protestant denominations, such as the Scottish Presbyterians and the English Puritans, went after Christmas with the same zeal with which Herod went after every boy under the age of two in Bethlehem. In Scotland, the holiday was so thoroughly suppressed from the late sixteenth century until the twentieth that most Scots had to work on December 25 into the 1960s, even after Christmas was declared a public holiday there in 1958. Although Christmas has made a comeback among the Scots, several of our New Year's celebrations, such as the countdown to midnight with a clock or singing "Auld Lang Syne," are from a time when Scotland's only major winter holiday was December 31–January 1.

In the seventeenth century the Puritans came very close to extirpating Christmas from the hearts of Englishmen. When Oliver Cromwell and his thugs came to power, they began passing laws against the observance of Christmas, forbidding church services and all other festivities, and mandating a fast on Christmas Day. When these edicts went largely ignored, they stepped up their game. The years from 1645 to 1647 were particularly tense: the Puritans launched a massive propaganda campaign against Christmas, and Parliament banned the holiday under pain of punishment. The result was great social unrest. Riots broke out across the country, Oxford was home to a "world of skull-breaking," and the mayor of Canterbury had his windows and his bones broken by a mob. But the Puritan-controlled government held firm, fining and imprisoning dissenters and firing ministers who decorated their churches for Christmas. Soldiers scoured the streets looking and smelling for any food that was being cooked for a Christmas dinner. Mincemeat pies, once baked to resemble Christ's cradle, were made illegal. As one critic lamented, the world had been turned upside down, but not in the playful topsy-turvy manner of medieval social inversion. The pearl-clutching, buzz-killing bad guys had won.

> Listen to me and you shall hear,
> News hath not been this thousand year:
> Since Herod, Caesar, and many more,
> You never heard the like before.
> > Holy-dayes are despis'd,
> > New fashions are devis'd.
> Old Christmas is kickt out of Town.
> > Yet let's be content, and the times lament,
> > You see the world turn'd upside down.[11]

Christmas returned to England with the Restoration of the monarchy in 1660, but it wasn't quite the same. Much of its sacred meaning and charitable outreach had been lost while only the feasting and revelries were retained. Whereas earlier English carols praised the Christ Child, songs from this era extolled "Minc'd pies and plum-porridge, Good ale and strong beer."[12] The English had brought back the bath water and forgotten about the Baby.

Cromwell and his ilk had their counterparts in the American colonies. The Pilgrims "celebrated" their first Christmas in 1620 by working as on any other day. Under Puritanical influence, the Massachusetts Bay Colony banned the holiday from 1659 to 1681, and even after that, December 25 remained a regular workday in Boston and the surrounding areas until 1856, when along with the Fourth of July and Washington's Birthday it was declared a public holiday. Before that, employers would often fire anyone who did not come to work that day, and some factory owners went so far as to move the start of the day shift to 5:00 a.m. or earlier on Christmas Day in order to keep their employees from attending morning Mass. As late as 1870, the Boston public school system held classes on December 25, and any student who played hooky was punished or expelled.[13] These measures were partially aimed at the city's growing Irish Catholic population, but it may have been German immigrants who ultimately softened the hearts of their neighbors. Louis Prang, father of the Christmas greeting card, was a member of Boston's only German Catholic parish, Holy Trinity German Church, where an outdoor Christmas children's pageant held in 1851 had to be repeated twice at the insistence of both Catholics and Protestants eager to see it (see Chapter Twelve). Boston went from being the most anti-Christmas city in the country to being the first city to have public Christmas trees, in 1912.

CHRISTKINDL, THE COMEBACK KID

As the history of Boston illustrates, it is hard to keep a good holiday down. In the nineteenth century, Christmas experienced a remarkable international revival and yet another transformation. As we will see in Chapter Four, American poets transformed St. Nicholas of Myra into the iconic Santa Claus (making the holiday more child-oriented), while on the other side of the Atlantic, Charles Dickens retrieved several cherished aspects of a traditional English Christmas as he too added a more family-centered focus. The American Civil War and its aftermath contributed to this domestication as families yearned to be reunited, forget about the horrors of war, and celebrate together (a pattern that would repeat during World War II with songs like "White Christmas"). In the late nineteenth century, advertisers got wise to the marketing potential of Christmas, and by the beginning of

Merry Old Santa Claus by Thomas Nast, who was instrumental in popularizing Santa Claus in the nineteenth century. *Harper's Weekly*

the twentieth century, writers were bemoaning the commercialization of Christmas—a lament that continues to this day.[14]

Christmas has always had its friends as well as its enemies. Today its friends worry about a new war on Christmas: an attempt to ban public symbols of the holiday and the greeting "Merry Christmas." A deeper problem, we suspect, is the difficulty of recapturing the original merriment, piety, and leisure of the holiday in so fast-paced and restless a society as ours. Here's hoping that the Ghost of Christmas Yet to Come is not as grim as he is in Dickens's Christmas carol about Scrooge.

Penne Restad, author of *Christmas in America*, is optimistic about the future, and so we will let her have the last word: "The durability of the American Christmas may, in fact, rest on its ability to bring to our material and scientific world, against daunting odds, a broadly shared hint of the sacred. It is in the brief December season that Americans, using the language and objects of their culture, recapture ideals and act according to their better selves. In this sense, the nation's Christmas truly brings together the culture's two most disparate yet similarly unbound projects—to seek wealth and to secure salvation."[15]

Chapter Two

THE BUILDUP: SOME COOL CUSTOMS OF ADVENT

Advent, the four-week period preceding Christmas, is a curious season. It awaits the coming of the Messiah, who already came two thousand years ago. It celebrates the first coming of Jesus Christ, who came in humility as a baby in Bethlehem, in order to prepare for His Second Coming, when He will come in glory as a Judge from the East. In churches, the penitential colors of violet and rose (okay, purple and pink) are used, and some hymns of joy (such as the *Gloria in excelsis*) are suppressed; meanwhile, outside churches, there are seasonal sweets and Yuletide drinks and radio stations playing Christmas music 24/7.

In nature, when a river empties into the ocean, it produces a brackish estuary in which only some creatures can survive. Advent is like that, a mixture of the fresh water of joy and the salt water of restraint, penance, and waiting. In these brackish waters dwell some wonderfully distinctive creatures. Here are a few examples.

ADVENT CALENDAR

A popular custom from nineteenth-century Lutheran Germany that heightens a sense of anticipation for Christmas is the Advent calendar. Advent calendars are usually colorful pieces of cardboard depicting a many-windowed house or scene. Behind each window is a picture or symbol that points to the coming of Christmas. The children are allowed to open one shutter a day until finally, on December 24, the front door of the house is opened to reveal the Nativity.

Numerous variations of the Advent calendar exist, some of them amusingly gluttonous, with shutters concealing chocolate, candy, or even tiny bottles of whiskey. Out of practicality, most Advent calendars begin on December 1 even though the date of the beginning of Advent varies from year to year. Homemade calendars, though, can be tailored to dates of the liturgical season for each year.

According to the *Guinness Book of World Records*, the largest Advent calendar, built at St. Pancras station in London in 2007, is over 23 stories high and 75 feet wide. The most valuable calendar, on the other hand, is estimated at $3.3 million. Crafted by Octagon Blue GVC in Belgium, it consists of 24 glass tubes that contain 124 diamonds wrapped in silver.[1]

ADVENT WREATH

The Advent wreath or Advent crown was invented by sixteenth-century Lutherans in east Germany. The wreath as we know it today, however, did not take shape until a nineteenth-century German Lutheran pastor named Johann Hinrich Wichern took an old cartwheel and attached to it twenty small red candles (symbolizing Saturdays and weekdays) and four large white candles (for the Sundays of Advent). Wichern had founded an orphanage, and to help the children experience the joy of the season, each day he lit a candle from the wreath, told them a story, and prayed with them.

After it was simplified into the four-candle wreath popular today, the custom spread to most Christian communities in Europe, Canada, and America, though not as fast as you might think—even into the 1940s it was virtually unknown in the United States. When the Von Trapp family (of *Sound of Music* fame) first arrived in America after escaping the Nazis and asked where they could obtain materials for their Advent wreath, they were met with blank stares.[2]

The custom itself is simple: a wreath made of evergreen is adorned with four candles equidistant from each other. The candles may be of any color: in some European countries they are white, in Germany they can be large and red, and in the U.S. they correspond to the liturgical colors of the four Sundays of Advent, three violet and one rose. The wreath can be suspended from the ceiling or placed in the center of a table. In a dark room, a violet candle is lit on the First Sunday of Advent, another on the Second, the rose candle on the Third (Gaudete Sunday), and the last candle on the Fourth Sunday.

Variations abound. One family places a large white "Christ candle" in the middle on Christmas Eve and lights it. Another removes the candles on Christmas Eve and converts their Advent wreath into a Christmas door wreath.

The symbolism of the Advent wreath is simple and effective. The wreath's circular shape recalls the crown of Christ the King or the eternity of the Trinity and betokens the "fullness of time" when God sent His son Jesus to redeem us (Galatians 4:4). The evergreen is an ancient symbol of hope and everlasting life. And the candles represent the hearts of the faithful burning for their Savior as well as the light of the prophets whose inspired words pierced the darkness in which mankind was enveloped while waiting for the Messiah.

Several municipalities vie for the honor of having the largest Advent wreath. Mariazell, Austria, boasts of the world's largest hanging Advent wreath, which is suspended in its town square.[3] In 2017, 300 volunteers in Mosnang, Switzerland, took 10,600 cubic feet of pinewood and built a wreath with a diameter of 393 feet and 4 electric red candles, each 19 feet high. Inside the wreath were a food stand and an ice-skating rink.[4] The people of Kaufbeuren, Germany, say that they have the world's largest (recurring) Advent wreath made from real fir branches, which they put up every year around their Neptune fountain. The wreath, which has been the city's trademark since about 2005, weighs two tons, has a diameter of over 26 feet, and features 4 stout pink candles that are almost 2 feet high.[5]

BARBARA BRANCHES (DECEMBER 4)

The virgin and martyr St. Barbara (ca. 200) is the patron saint of artillerymen, miners, and a happy death. A "Barbara branch" is a twig broken from a fruit tree (especially cherry), placed in a bowl of water on her feast day of December 4, and kept in a warm and well-lit place. According to legend, if the Barbara branch blooms on or before Christmas Day, it will bring good luck. The custom was once particularly popular among maidens seeking a husband.

Besides this harmless superstition, Barbara branches are reminiscent of the image from Isaiah of Christ as a branch from the root of Jesse (Isaiah 11.2); they can thus be instructive in teaching children the meaning of Advent and Christmas. Barbara branches are also used as a tribute to the Christ Child in the manger, lovingly placed in or near the crèche when they have blossomed.

By the way, you can also call St. Barbara the patron saint of barbiturates, since they were named after her, thanks to a strange accident of history. When German chemist Adolf von Baeyer invented the compound from which the drugs derive, he and his colleagues went to celebrate at a tavern where the local artillery garrison happened to be celebrating St. Barbara's Day. One of the officers suggested Barbara's name for the new substance and Baeyer, perhaps his judgment affected by a pint or two, agreed.

GOLDEN NIGHTS AND O COME, O COME, EMMANUEL (DECEMBER 17–23)

If you have ever wondered about the inspiration behind the beloved Advent hymn "O Come, O Come, Emmanuel," wonder no more. Beginning on December 17 and ending on the evening of December 23, Catholics, Anglicans, Episcopalians, and a growing number of other Christians use seven special antiphons for the office of Vespers or Evensong that call upon Jesus Christ under a different title each night: "O Wisdom," "O Adonai," "O Root of Jesse," "O Key of David," "O Dayspring," "O King of the Nations," and "O

Emmanuel." Together these different "O Antiphons" retrace the influence of the Son of God on sacred history even before He became Incarnate.

The antiphons are also noteworthy for their "secret code." Take the first letter of the Latin titles from each antiphon (Sapientia, Adonai, Radix, Clavis, Oriens, Rex, Emmanuel), and you will see that they form an acrostic that, when read backward, spells *ERO CRAS*—Latin for "I will be [there] tomorrow." It is as if Christ is answering our prayers through the very prayer itself.

The period of the O Antiphons, called the Golden Nights or Sapientiatide (Wisdom Tide), is a time of heightened anticipation of the Lord's coming. The joy was so irrepressible that the salutation "Keep your O" was common in several medieval monasteries—an admonition that always makes us chuckle, perhaps because we imagine its being voiced in an ultra-cool Barry White bass.

In the medieval cloister the Golden Nights were often marked by little treats. According to Maria von Trapp, on the day when Christ was called the "Root of Jesse," Brother Gardener would bring out "his choicest vegetables and fruits, with specially beautiful roots among them." And on the day when Christ was invoked as the "Key of David," Brother Cellarer "used his key for the wine cellar and brought out the best wine."[6]

In many places, this octave of preparation was extended over nine days, making a Novena. In the Alps, schoolchildren observed the custom of *Josephstragen*, "carrying St. Joseph." Each night a group of boys would carry a statue of St. Joseph to another boy's home. The night after the visit, the boy who had been visited would join the procession, swelling the number of carriers. On Christmas Eve all the boys, accompanied by schoolgirls dressed in white, would process the statue through the town to the church, where it would be placed near the manger.

In Latin America, a Novena to the Holy Child (*La Novena del Niño*) can consist of praying and singing lively carols in front of the church's empty manger. The devotion began in the late eighteenth century and continues to the present day.

JESSE TREE

Although the Jesse Tree is a fairly recent custom, its roots (pun intended) go back to the twelfth century, when elaborate family trees of Jesus Christ graced the stained-glass windows of cathedrals like Our Lady of Chartres. The tree takes its name from King David's father, Jesse of Bethlehem, and is inspired by Isaiah 11:1—"there shall come forth a rod out of the root of Jesse, and a flower shall rise up out of his root," and by Isaiah 11:10—"In that day the root of Jesse, who standeth for an ensign of the people, him the Gentiles shall beseech." In the Gospel according to St. Matthew, the genealogy of Jesus Christ is divided into three sets of ancestors, fourteen generations apiece, and traditionally the Jesse tree roughly follows the last two sets, from the birth of David to the Babylonian captivity and from the captivity to the birth of the Savior (Matthew 1:1–17).

The modern Jesse tree, which is little more than a generation old, can be a poster, a small bush (real or artificial), or a bare branch such as mesquite either wedged into a pot or fixed into the cross section of a log. On the tree are placed symbols of Christ's ancestors, beginning with Jesse or even Adam—either all at once or one per night. Another option is to decorate the tree with symbols of Jesus Christ, especially the titles of Our Lord as they appear in the O Antiphons of the Golden Nights. The O Antiphons can be found in the verses of the hymn "O Come, O Come, Emmanuel"—they just need to be rearranged in chronological order, from the "Wisdom on High" in Genesis to "Emmanuel" in Isaiah. Beginning on December 17, the family sings the appropriate verse of the hymn while the corresponding symbol is put on the tree; each night a new verse and a new symbol are added, so that by December 23, the entire hymn is sung and all the symbols used. Depending on their relative sizes, the Jesse tree can be placed in the middle of the Advent wreath and then replaced with the Christ candle on December 24 as a way of signifying how the figures have yielded to the reality.

LUCY LIGHTS AND DELIGHTS (DECEMBER 13)

St. Lucy's Day celebration. *Adèle Söderberg*

The customs for St. Lucy's Day on December 13 also illuminate the meaning of Advent and Christmas. St. Lucy was a virgin and martyr from Syracuse, Italy, who was beheaded in A.D. 304. Lucy's name means light, and this association has made her the patron saint of occupations requiring artificial light (such as writers and seamstresses) and of occupations communicating light, such as stained-glass making and glazing. Lucy is also the patron saint of eyes (the "light of the body") and of eye-care specialists such as opticians and ophthalmologists. Reinforcing this patronage is a legend that Lucy's eyes were gouged out by her pagan Roman torturers but miraculously grew back later that night. Before the Gregorian reform of the calendar in 1582, the saint's feast day fell on the shortest day of the year, the winter solstice.

For all these reasons, St. Lucy is honored on December 13 with a number of customs involving fire. Lucy candles were once lit in the home and Lucy fires burned outside. In Sweden and Norway, a girl dressed in white and wearing an evergreen wreath on her head with lit candles awakens the family and offers them coffee and cakes. She is called the *Lussibrud* (Lucy bride) and her pastry is *Lussekattor*. Today, Swedes use safer versions of the St. Lucia crown, with batteries instead of flames.

The Feast of St. Lucy comes at a good time, approximately halfway through the observance of Advent. The light of St. Lucy foreshadows the coming of the Light of the World on December 25 like a ray we can follow back to the sun.

NATIVITY SCENE

The Nativity scene or crèche arose out of ancient piety and medieval theater. Christians were honoring the cave in Bethlehem where Jesus Christ is believed to have been born even before St. Helen built the Basilica of the Nativity over it around A.D. 330 (she also allegedly discovered remains of the true Crib, which are now in the basilica St. Mary Major in Rome). Medieval mystery plays later reenacted the Nativity, but when they got out of hand they were suppressed.

A generation later, however, St. Francis of Assisi obtained papal permission to stage a live outdoor Nativity scene. On Christmas Eve 1223, in a cave in Greccio, Italy, the saint had a manger set up with hay and a live ox and donkey. Then, during a Solemn High Mass, his cheeks bathed in tears of joy, he sang the Gospel and preached on the "Nativity of the poor King and the humble town of Bethlehem."

The Gospel accounts of Christ's birth do not mention what animals if any were in the stable at the time, but

Christians applied Isaiah 1:3 to the birth of the Messiah: "The ox knoweth his owner, and the ass his master's crib: but Israel hath not known me, and my people hath not understood." A sarcophagus from A.D. 385 depicts the Christ Child between an ox and a donkey—without Joseph and Mary! The early Church was also influenced by an old Latin translation of Habakkuk 3:2 "In the midst of two animals Thou shalt become known."

St. Francis's idea caught on quickly throughout Western Christendom, first in churches and then in homes. Not even the Reformation, with its rejection of "graven images," could dislodge some Germans from their Nativity scenes: they would rather be bad Protestants than be bereft of their crèches. It was most likely Germans who brought the first Nativity scenes to the United States.

A Nativity scene can be a *tableau vivant* involving live actors and animals, like St. Francis's original reenactment. The record for the world's largest of these was set in Provo, Utah, in 2014 and involved 1,039 volunteers, most of them dressed as angels.[7] More common are nativity sets of model figures. The world's smallest crèche was created with 3-D printing by scientists at Vilnius University in imitation of the Nativity scene at Cathedral Square in Vilnius, Lithuania. Called "The Nano Holy Family," it is ten thousand times smaller than the original and invisible to the naked eye. The entire microscopic model, which took thirty experts three months to make, can fit through the eye of a needle or on an eyelash; the Infant

Jesus is smaller than a human cell.[8] At the other end of the spectrum, Alicante, Spain, boasts the world's largest Nativity figures: Baby Jesus is over ten feet high, ten feet wide, and thirteen feet long, Joseph is over fifty-nine feet high, and Mary is almost thirty-five feet.[9]

The simplest Nativity scenes have only the Holy Family of Jesus, Mary, and Joseph, but it is more common to have all the principal characters of the Christmas story, such as angels, shepherds, the Magi, and an ox and an ass. Crèches can be quite elaborate: Some depict entire modern cities, villages, or castles. In 2017, the townsfolk of Aubagne, France, put up a crèche that covered 1,615 square feet and featured 3,500 figurines ranging from the Holy Family to people in a French post office, cinema, and bar.[10]

There are a number of charming customs involving the crèche. One is not to place the Infant Jesus in the manger until Christmas morning or after Midnight Mass to heighten anticipation. Another is to have the family's children prepare the manger by earning wisps of straw that can be used for the Infant Jesus' bedding; they earn the straw by prayers or good works. This custom, which began long ago in France, teaches children that the cultivation of virtue is the best way to prepare for the Lord's coming.

Third, the figurines for the Three Kings can be placed at the opposite end of the room and moved a little closer to the manger scene (either with the help of the children or "miraculously" while they sleep) every day during Advent and the Twelve Days of Christmas until they arrive at their destination on January 6, the Feast of the Epiphany.

A similar practice can be implemented with the figurines of Joseph and Mary, to symbolize their journey from Galilee to Bethlehem; of course they need to arrive by December 24. On Christmas morning, the children awaken to the sight of Baby Jesus in the manger surrounded by His loving parents.

PLUM PUDDING

Anglicans and Episcopalians call the Sunday before Advent "Stir Up Sunday" and use the day to begin stirring up their Christmas or plum pudding (which takes weeks to mature properly). On the other hand, and for historical reasons that are unclear, Catholics call the First Sunday of Advent "Stir Up Sunday" and begin their puddings on that day. Both Sundays are appropriate, insofar as each has a collect (or entrance prayer) that opens with the words "Stir up, we beseech Thee, O Lord."[11]

The process of making a traditional Christmas pudding has come to be steeped in allegory and harmless superstition. It should be stirred from East to West to commemorate the journey

Mrs. Cratitch appears with the plum pudding "bedight with Christmas holly." *Sol Eytinge Jr.*

of the Magi; it should have thirteen ingredients in honor of Christ and His Apostles; and every member of the family and every guest should stir the pudding while making a secret wish. The stirring represents the arousal of our hearts for the Lord's coming, while the richness of the pudding represents the good things that He brings with Him from Heaven. There is even a little poem to accompany the task:

> Stir up, we beseech thee,
> The pudding in the pot;
> And when we get home
> We'll eat the lot.

Christmas pudding may also include good luck tokens, such as a coin for prosperity, a thimble for luck—or another year of spinsterhood!—a button for another year of bachelorhood, and a ring for marriage, with each of these blessings going to the person who finds the relevant object in his piece. Just make certain to tell everyone to look for them, so that no one will choke on his new destiny.

As for the more edible side of the pudding, ingredients include currants, sultanas or raisins, sugar, lemon rind, nutmeg, cinnamon, breadcrumbs, eggs, and suet (because the latter is no longer common in U.S. grocery stores, American recipes usually call for butter instead). But the most famous addition is brandy, both as an ingredient and as a sauce: as an ingredient it keeps the pudding from getting moldy and as a sauce it is set ablaze after the pudding has been grandly presented to the family at the end of Christmas dinner. Several fine cookbooks, including *Feast Day Cookbook, Around the Year with the von Trapp Family, Family Advent Customs*, and *A Continual Feast* contain recipes for plum pudding, though I must confess that my favorite is Nigella Lawson's "Ultimate Christmas Pudding."[12]

ST. THOMAS THE APOSTLE (DECEMBER 21)

In the traditional Roman calendar, December 21 is the Feast of St. Thomas the Apostle. In 1969 the feast was moved to July 3, probably so as not to interfere with the season of Advent, but the traditional feast reinforces belief in the divinity of Jesus Christ, born in a manger. Hence the words of Dom Guéranger: "To none of the Apostles could this day have been so fittingly assigned as to St. Thomas. It was St. Thomas whom we needed; St. Thomas, whose festal patronage would aid us to believe and hope in that God whom we see not, and who comes to us in silence and humility in order to try our Faith. Saint Thomas…comes then most appropriately to defend us, by the power of his example and prayers, against the temptations which proud human reason might excite within us."[13]

The customs surrounding the old St. Thomas's Day are memorable. "Thomasing" was an eighteenth- and nineteenth-century English custom in which impoverished widows went from house to house begging for milk, wheat, oatmeal, or flour in order to make treats for Christmas.[14] In some parts of Central Europe, St. Thomas's feast began the period of the "Rough Nights," when country folk would use grotesque masks and loud noises such as the cracking of whips and the ringing of bells to drive away demons in preparation for Christmas. A more pious strategy involved farmers and their sons' walking around their land with incense and holy water while the rest of the family recited the rosary.[15]

In Norway, all Yuletide preparations—chopping firewood, baking, and slaughtering—had to be completed by St. Thomas's Day so that one could spend the last few days before Christmas getting into a more spiritual frame of mind. The Apostle even took on the nickname "St. Thomas the Brewer" because all holiday beer had to be brewed by December 21 (and no more brewing could be done until after Epiphany). Norwegians once visited each other on St. Thomas's Day to sample each other's Christmas ale.

December 21 in Norway also marked the beginning of the "Peace of Christmas," which endeavored to maintain Christian concord during this sacred season. The Peace was taken seriously: penalties for acts of violence were doubled, and some people even went so far as to avoid mentioning the names of harmful animals.

St. Thomas's feast was also known in some parts as "Spinning Night" because women stayed up late into the night spinning thread to pay for Christmas expenses, their labors lightened by dancing and singing. "St. Thomas's Dole," a kind of Christmas bonus, helped employees and the needy make ends meet during the holiday season.

And possibly because December 21 is the winter solstice, the feast attracted some rather comical divination practices.[16] In Germany, if a girl slept on this day with her feet on the pillow and her head at the foot of the bed, she would be given a glimpse of her future husband in a dream. In England, the same goal was achieved by wrapping an onion in a handkerchief and placing it under one's pillow. Meanwhile, if a German baker stopped kneading the dough for *Kletzenbrot* or *Hutzelbrot* to run out and hug the trees in the orchard, they were guaranteed to bear much fruit in the coming year.[17]

Chapter Three

THE REAL ST. NICK

I n the last chapter we touched on several Advent customs for saints' feast days, but we left out the most famous saint of the season. St. Nicholas of Myra (270–343), whose feast is celebrated on December 6, is the second most popular patron saint in the world, chalking up more patronages than any other holy figure besides the Blessed Virgin Mary. And yet his biography is considered so unreliable that his feast was demoted to an optional memorial by the Catholic Church in 1969. "Though one of the most popular saints in both the Greek and Latin Churches," concludes *The Oxford Dictionary of the Christian*

Church, "scarcely anything is historically certain about him."[1]

We can understand the skepticism. Long before he became "Santa Claus," St. Nicholas was a magnet for misappropriation and colorful imagination. Legends about the saint were already growing in the first millennium, when the legends of *another* saint were grafted onto his. In the tenth century, the aptly named Symeon "Metaphrastes" (the "compiler" or "paraphraser") combined the stories of the original St. Nicholas with St. Nicholas of Sion, a monk who had died in 564, almost two centuries after the bishop of Myra. And in the second millennium, medieval Christians took the St. Nicholas story in directions that would have had even Symeon rubbing his eyes in disbelief.

But certainty can be surprisingly fickle. While the sophisticated position has been to doubt Nicholas's dossier, more recent scholarship is changing the conversation about the holy bishop whom the Eastern Churches continue to revere as Nicholas the Wonderworker. By following these new threads, we can arrive at a fairly reliable profile of this popular saint.

DEFENDER OF FAMILY VALUES

Nicholas was born in Patara, a coastal town in the Lycia region of southwest Asia Minor (present-day Turkey). When he was eighteen his wealthy parents died, and after the pious Nicholas asked God what to do with the fortune, he learned of a heartbreaking case. A nobleman who lived not far from him had fallen into destitution through the machinations of Satan. The Devil's goal was to induce the man into abandoning God and sinning, and it worked: unable to marry off his three daughters without a dowry, the man decided to sell them into prostitution.

This shocking decision was not uncommon in antiquity. The Emperor Constantine made public funds available in limited areas to assist impoverished families so that they would not contemplate selling their children into slavery or prostitution, and the Church excommunicated fathers who abused their parental rights in this manner.

But the sad practice continued. In a sermon, a traumatized St. Basil the Great describes witnessing a father in the marketplace selling his children to pay off his debt, and St. Ambrose describes the pain of a father who must choose between handing his children over to the slave trader or starving to death.[2]

Enter St. Nicholas. The holy layman threw three bags (actually, wrapped-up cloths) of gold coins through the window of the man's house so that he would be able to afford a respectable marriage for his daughters. Some variations of the story condense Nicholas's actions into three consecutive nights, but according to our earliest account Nicholas, a wise and prudent donor who was concerned about the spiritual and temporal effects of his charity, waited to see what the man would do with the first bag. Happily, the man immediately procured a marriage for his eldest daughter, and he did the same thing for his second daughter after Nicholas anonymously gave him another bag.

Nicholas's generosity not only saved the family from sinning, it restored their faith in God as well. After his first two daughters were married, the father prayed to God to know the identity of the man who had been so kind to them, and God answered his prayer: the father was able to catch Nicholas in the act the third time, and to thank him personally. Falling to his knees, the man would have kissed Nicholas's feet had the saint not prevented him. Nicholas helped him off the ground and made him swear never to tell a soul about what had happened.

Nicholas's generosity is an implicit affirmation of what today are called family values. Even though Nicholas himself would choose celibacy, his kindness underscores the goodness of marriage and family, both of which are worth fighting (or sacrificing) for. Understandably, Nicholas became the patron saint of the poor, prostitutes, brides, and newlyweds. And because he used money to save the family, he is a patron saint of bankers, merchants, and pawnbrokers. In fact, pawnbrokers liked Nicholas so much that they made three bags of coins the symbol of their guild. To this day, three circles are the symbol of a pawn shop.

BISHOP OF MYRA

Nicholas afterwards became a cleric of some sort (probably a priest, but we are not sure). When the bishop of Myra died, Nicholas journeyed the twenty miles from his hometown of Patara to pay his respects. Unbeknownst to him, neighboring bishops had gathered in the church at Myra to elect and consecrate a new bishop. Candidates for the position were not exactly plentiful: the Church was still being persecuted by the Roman Empire, and bishops could expect imprisonment, torture, or execution.

In desperation, the bishops agreed to elect the first man who walked into the church that day. When Nicholas crossed the threshold, a bishop asked him, "Son, what is your name?" "Sir," he replied, "I am the sinner Nicholas, a servant of Your Excellency." Nicholas's humility astonished all who heard him, and the bishop said, "Son, come with me." They consecrated him a bishop then and there.

It was rare for someone to be made a bishop so young (Nicholas was between thirty and thirty-five), but sudden ordination was not unheard of. St. Ambrose went from being a *catechumen* (an unbaptized Christian candidate) to a bishop in a breathtaking nine days, and St. Augustine was forcibly made a priest when others noticed that he was in the congregation and implored the bishop to ordain him immediately.

Nicholas barely had time to settle into his new job before he was arrested, imprisoned, and tortured. It was common at the time to blind the right eye and to cut the sinews of the left ankle of steadfast Christians,[3] but we do not know if Nicholas suffered such a plight. One biographer only relates that at the Council of Nicaea, many bishops had scars from the time of persecution, especially Nicholas and one other.

In 1953, a forensic investigation of what is believed to be the skull of St. Nicholas in the cathedral of Bari, Italy, revealed that the nose had been badly broken. The breakage may have happened post-mortem when sloppy merchants from Bari looted—er, transferred—the relics of St. Nicholas to their native city in 1087. But if it did not, the condition of the nose could be confirmation of Nicholas's rough treatment in prison—or, as we are about to see, it could lend support to a story about a pugilistic Nicholas's striking the heretic Arius.

DECK THE HERETIC?

It is likely that Nicholas was one of three hundred bishops who attended the Council of Nicaea in A.D. 325.[4] There is a medieval legend that when Arius the Alexandrian priest took the floor and went on and on about how Jesus Christ was *not* consubstantial with the Father, Nicholas, unable to bear Arius's heretical prattling any longer, walked up to him and slapped him. (As one meme puts it, "Deck the halls? How about deck the heretic?")

The story goes on to assert that Nicholas was imprisoned for striking a bishop, but that that night Jesus Christ and the Blessed Virgin Mary visited him in jail, congratulated him for defending the truth, and liberated him.

Nicholas's earliest biographer, however, paints a different picture, one more consistent with the saint's famous kindness. According to Michael the Archimandrite, Nicholas exuded such an odor of sanctity that his mere appearance made others better. And he was so concerned about the welfare of others that he pressured heretics to be better too. Theognis was the bishop of Nicaea and a major player at the Council; he was also the kind of man who "irritated everyone with his stubbornness."[5] Theognis had reluctantly signed on to the orthodox position as formulated by the Council, but when the emperor announced that Arius would be excommunicated and exiled, Theognis angrily protested against what in his opinion was an excessive punishment. No paragon of patience himself, the emperor quickly procured Theognis's excommunication. The standoff was resolved by St. Nicholas, who gently urged his colleague to do the right thing through a series of letters. It worked, and Theognis submitted himself to the judgment of the Council when it convened again in 327.

REGIONAL EXORCIST

Nicholas's early biographers describe him as expelling many demons by destroying pagan shrines and groves, including Myra's great temple dedicated to Artemis (Diana). The early Church took seriously Psalm 95:5 (96:5)—"All the gods of the gentiles are devils"—and treated the Greco-Roman deities as demons in disguise. A biography of St. Martin of Tours, who lived a generation after Nicholas on the other (western) side of the Empire, relates that when demons who were possessing someone revealed their name, it was the name of a pagan god like Jove or Mercury.[6] Christianity went from being a religion with two million adherents when he was born to a religion of thirty-four million when he passed away, but the old religion was still alive and well during his lifetime, and the old habits died hard. Christians were often the victims of mob violence, but sometimes they fought back, applying to their own situation Matthew 3:10— "the axe is laid to the root of the tree." An early coin from Myra depicts the goddess Artemis crouched in the branches of a tree with two men standing below with raised axes.[7]

Nicholas's protection of his flock from the demonic only grew after his death. According to a legend first recorded in the early eighth century, a demon bent on retribution for Nicholas's victories disguised itself as a little old lady and persuaded pilgrims sailing to Myra to bring with them a small flask of oil for the lamps of the saint's tomb. The flask, however, was a bomb with properties similar to the Byzantine secret weapon "Greek fire." That night one of the pilgrims was warned in a dream to throw it into the sea, and when he did, it exploded and caused a series of waves that threatened to capsize the ship. Suddenly, Nicholas himself appeared and calmed the waters. To this day St. Nicholas is a patron of travelers, pilgrims, and all those tied to the sea, including but not limited to sailors, fishermen, longshoremen, maritime pilots, and the Greek Navy. There was a time when churches dedicated to the saint would be built along the shore so that they could be seen off the coast as landmarks.

THE GO-TO GUY

It is tempting to think of patron saints as "replacements" of the Roman gods, with specific saints replacing specific gods for specific causes in a sort of watered-down monotheism for recovering polytheists. This theory has the right location but the wrong target. It was not the Roman pantheon but the Roman patron-client relationship that served as the inspiration for saintly patronage. In this important relationship, the client owed the patron honor and gifts while the patron owed the client certain favors, such as helping him find a job. A "patron" was a boss or big shot who had your back; he was the go-to guy when you got in trouble. Think of it as a legal and moral version of *The Godfather* movies, with all the big fat Italian weddings but without all the sleeping with the fishes.

Patronages on earth were especially important in the third and fourth centuries, when the imperial regime became increasingly swamped by Big Government expenses and corrupt officials. In response, common folk turned more and more to bishops to protect them, for bishops had legal and moral leverage against local government officials and were far more trustworthy.

Even before his death, Nicholas was looked to as a patron. When the government imposed a burdensome new tax, Nicholas personally appealed to the Emperor Constantine in Constantinople to have it greatly reduced. And because Nicholas was nobody's fool, he miraculously sent the signed decree back to Myra before the emperor could regret his decision (which he soon did).

Early in his life, when three young men were about to be executed by the corrupt local governor, Nicholas stopped the execution and confronted the official, who subsequently confessed that he had been bribed. This amazing intervention left a deep impression on three witnesses, military officers named Nepotianus, Ursus, and Eupoleonis, and when they later returned to Constantinople and found themselves falsely accused of high treason, it was Nicholas to whom they turned. Imprisoned and awaiting execution in the morning, they cried out to the God of Nicholas for help. That night Nicholas appeared to the Emperor Constantine in a dream, chided him for his rashness, and demanded the release of the officers. After Nicholas threatened to serve Constantine's remains to vultures if he did not comply (!), the emperor asked him who he was. "I am Bishop Nicholas, a sinner," he replied. Constantine awoke and summoned his consul, who had had the same dream. Now truly frightened, the emperor summoned the three men and asked them if they had heard of someone named Nicholas. The officers rejoiced at the mention of his name, and the emperor, sensing the hand of God, released them immediately.

The story of Nepotianus, Ursus, and Eupoleonis is one of the earliest that we have of the saint, but over time it turned into quite a different tale. In a later iteration, the three men, clerics rather than soldiers, were murdered by an innkeeper for their money and resurrected by Nicholas. From there the tale grew outrageously: the three were now boys, and the wicked innkeeper murdered them, dismembered them, and pickled their remains in a barrel or brine tub. According to this version, Nicholas reassembled and resurrected the boys after forcing the innkeeper to repent. Because of this gruesome tale, Nicholas posthumously took on additional jobs as patron of coopers/barrel-makers, poor boys such as boot blacks (shoeshiners), repentant murderers, innkeepers, restaurateurs, and brewers (who make the most popular item on an inn's menu).

Even among the usual game-of-telephone distortions that happen over time, the transformation of three Roman generals into three pickled boys stands out. One interesting catalyst may have been bad art. According to one theory, depictions of the three officers stretching out their arms from a barred window in a prison tower may have been misinterpreted by confused spectators as like-nesses of three boys in a barrel.[8] According to another, the three bags of coins betokening a pawnshop could have been mistaken for the heads of three children![9]

Whatever its origin, the innkeeper story sealed the saint's reputation as a patron of youth, which in turn led to the composition of more stories and more patronages. To give one example: Nicholas is said to have appeared in a dream to two juvenile delinquents and shown them the impact of their thieving on the lives of their victims. Consequently, the holy bishop became a patron saint of repentant thieves.

And since we are on the theme of patronages, we will mention two more. Because his relics continue to this day to secrete a fragrant and healing oil called "myrrh" or "manna," Nicholas is the patron saint of oil merchants and perfumers.

FEAST DAYS

St. Nicholas traditionally enjoys two feast days: December 6, which commemorates his death and which has been on the universal calendar for centuries, and May 9, which commemorates the translation of his relics to Bari and appears on local calendars. We are not certain why December 6 was chosen. It could have been the actual date that Nicholas passed away, but since December 6 was an important date in the port town of Myra, there may have been an ulterior motive. As the symbolic beginning of winter, December 6 marked the occasion when sacrifices were made to the goddess Artemis, protectress of seafarers, for all those who would dare the Mediterranean during the dangerous winter months. After Nicholas destroyed the temple of Artemis, it was only natural that he would take on some of her responsibilities—not as a god or a substitute for God, but as a friend of both God and the people.[10]

But a more striking explanation of the dates is from a Russian folktale. Once upon a time, a peasant's cart became mired in the mud on a lonely road. Saint Cassian passed by, but when the peasant asked for help, the saint declined, not wishing to soil his heavenly robes. Next came St. Nicholas, and when the peasant asked for help, Nicholas immediately leapt to his aid. After Cassian and Nicholas returned to heaven, God noticed that the latter's robes were caked in mud. Rather than be upset, He gave Nicholas two feasts a year and assigned Cassian's feast, on the other hand, to February 29, which occurs once every four years.[11]

ASSESSMENT

It is impossible to know with absolute certainty what Nicholas of Myra did and did not do. Although Nicholas's praises were sung in writing as early as the late fourth century (not long after his death in 343), the first full-fledged biography of him did not appear until A.D. 710.[12] Nevertheless, the early accounts of his life that we have are topographically accurate about the region where he lived[13] and, as we have seen, culturally correct.

Adam English offers a useful metaphor for the best way to approach the stories of St. Nicholas. In 1553 monks from the Monastery of Stavronikita on Mount Athos were fishing in the sea when their net dredged up a mosaic icon of St. Nicholas that had an oyster lodged in the forehead (monks had allegedly thrown icons into the sea centuries earlier to protect them from Iconoclasts). When the monks dislodged the oyster, the icon was disfigured and began to bleed. Getting to the "truth" about St. Nicholas, English opines, is like that. He writes, "The barnacles of legend, myth, and exaggeration that have cemented themselves to the historical facts must be pried away. And yet, it should be kept in mind that the folkloric barnacles cannot be detached without permanently scarring—or even losing—the person. They are too tightly joined."[14] Perhaps the solution is the one devised by the monks of Stavronikita. They venerate "St. Nicholas of the Oyster" (*Agios Nikolaos o Streidas*) as a miraculous icon, on which dried blood may still be seen. But they also cherish the two shells of the oyster, having turned them into sacred vessels.

Finally, it is well to ponder one intriguing piece of circumstantial evidence about Nicholas of Myra. Appropriately, Nicholas means "victory of the people." Prior to the fourth century the name was rare, but after the fourth century it was common, beginning in Nicholas's home region of Lycia and then spreading to the rest of Asia Minor, Constantinople, Greece, and beyond. Could it be that the people, recognizing Nicholas as their champion, gratefully named their children after him in ever increasing numbers?[15]

Chapter Four

APPLE-CHEEKED TRANS-FORMATION: THE CUSTOMS OF ST. NICHOLAS AND THE BIRTH OF SANTA CLAUS

I
f you think that St. Nicholas was transformed into Santa Claus because of his enormous popularity as a patron saint, you are partly right. St. Nick was indeed so popular that his memory stayed alive even in strongly Protestant countries like Holland. But it is two stories in particular from the biography of St. Nicholas that inspired the customs which eventually gave us, with a lot of cross-pollination, the modern Santa Claus myth.

BOY BISHOP

The first story concerns Nicholas's age when he was consecrated a bishop. According to his earliest biographer, Nicholas was around thirty when he was given this honor—after he happened to be the first person who walked into the church that day. Usually only much older men were ordained bishop, and so Nicholas's relative youth fired the medieval imagination and led to the survival of the custom of the Boy Bishop.

We say survival rather than establishment because from what we can tell, the custom of a boy's impersonating a bishop began with devotion to Pope St. Gregory the Great (d. 600). St. Gregory is the patron saint of choirboys, and on his feast day (March 12), a young chorister would be chosen to represent him. The lad, festooned in pontifical robes, would preside over a service, appoint two of his peers as "chaplains," interrogate both adults and children about their catechism, and even give a sermon.[1]

After the Feast of the Holy Innocents on December 28 became a feast day for choirboys and students in the eleventh century, the Boy Bishop custom naturally migrated from March to that date. Our earliest mention of *a* Boy Bishop during Christmastime is from the Abbey of St. Gall in Switzerland. A boy dressed in the vestments of a bishop and accompanied by young classmates dressed as priests presided over Solemn Vespers. King Conrad I came to the abbey to observe this custom in A.D. 912, and he decided to test the boys' resolve by having apples strewn along the aisle of the church. He was impressed when not even the tiniest lad broke ranks from the procession to grab one.[2]

Originally the Boy Bishop custom was meant to foster vocations to the priesthood by giving youngsters a taste of liturgical officiating, but once it moved to within the Twelve Days of Christmas, it became linked with more riotous, topsy-turvy customs like the Feast of the Ass or the Lord of Misrule. In an effort to put an end to this nonsense, Church authorities decided to move the custom to the Feast of St. Nicholas on December 6, safely out of the way of Christmas.[3] But the plan backfired. Instead of stemming abuses, it extended them: the Boy Bishop would now preside from December 6 to December 28! And the practice was spreading. Initially it was associated only with cathedrals (which by definition have a presiding bishop), but over time other churches took up the practice. Even prestigious institutions such as Eton in England had a Boy Bishop.

From Italy to Scandinavia and from Ireland to Hungary, medieval Christians relished the Boy Bishop or Nicholas Bishop (as he came to be called), who solemnly processed through the town with his entourage blessing the crowds. We still have inventory records of the little vestments kept for the occasion. And although complaints continued to pour in about abuses (not unlike their adult counterparts, the boys sometimes emptied the church kitty to fuel their merriment), there was a touching side as well. When a Boy Bishop in the diocese of Salisbury died during his brief appointment, he was given the full funeral of a bishop and buried in the cathedral.

Eventually, authorities began to crack down. In 1541, King Henry VIII outlawed the practice as superstitious and pagan. Queen Mary brought the Boy Bishop back, but after Elizabeth's accession he fell into disfavor again; by the seventeenth century he was an extinct species in England. In 1982, however, the Anglican cathedral in Hereford resurrected the Boy Bishop, who again presides over some services from December 6 to 28 and gives a sermon. He is installed in a memorable way: during the celebration of Evensong or Vespers when the Magnificat is sung, the bishop of Hereford rises from his episcopal throne at the verse "He hath put down the mighty from their seat." Then, the boy, dressed in the regalia of a bishop, takes his seat at the verse "And He hath exalted the humble" and is given the bishop's crozier. Whatever effect this inversion has for the boy, it must surely be good for the bishop.

Some Catholics on the Continent began distancing themselves from this custom in the fifteenth and sixteenth centuries, although it survived in places like Lyons and Rheims, France, into the eighteenth. In Central Europe and Holland, the Boy Bishop did not disappear but grew up. Adults began to impersonate the bishop, and some believe that it is this maturation of the custom that led to the famous annual visit of St. Nick.[4] Now, however, the bishop does not lead in prayer but in gift-giving, thanks to the story about Nicholas's tossing bags of coins into a poor man's window so that his daughters could be married (see Chapter Three).

VISIT OF ST. NICHOLAS

The Visit of St. Nicholas is the most popular and recognizable custom associated with his feast day. In some places, children write notes addressed to the Child Jesus and put them on their windowsill on the night of December 5 for St. Nicholas to carry to Heaven. A more common custom is for children to leave their stockings or shoes near the fireplace in the hope that St. Nicholas will fill them with treats: chocolate coins are a popular option today, as they hark back to the story of the poor man and his daughters.

But the greatest honor of all is to have the saint visit the children while they are awake. Dressed in the rich vestments of a bishop, a white-bearded St. Nicholas asks the children questions about their prayers or behavior and admonishes them to have a holy Advent and Christmas. He then distributes little treats such as fruit or candy and "departs with a kindly farewell, leaving the little ones filled with holy awe."[5]

Or else he promises to return the next morning. In Holland, children stuff their shoes with hay or carrots for Nicholas's beautiful white horse Schimmel and place them near the fireplace. If they have been good, they discover in the morning that the fodder has been replaced by treats and toys; if they have not, the fodder is left untouched and the only gift is a rod.[6] In Tyrol, Austria, children wisely ditch the milk and cookies and leave out a glass of schnapps for St. Nicholas's servant. (I guess St. Nicholas is the designated driver).

Francis X. Weiser, a priest who was born in Vienna in 1901 and the author of *The Christmas Book*, has this to say about the visit of St. Nicholas:

> I still vividly remember the annual visit of this friendly and saintly figure on the evening of December 5. With joy and happy excitement we awaited his coming. We were convinced, as little children easily are, that he really was our great Patron Saint who came from Heaven on his feast day to visit us children whom he loved so much. With utter sincerity we promised him to overcome our faults, to obey our parents and to prepare our hearts for Christmas. Gratefully we accepted his gifts and kissed the ring on his holy hand. Never again in all my life have I experienced the unspeakable thrill of a physical nearness to Heaven as I did on those evenings of my childhood when "St. Nicholas" came to us. When I later found out that it was not really the Saint but a man representing him, this caused me no shock or harm. The thrill I

had felt remained in my memory and has
remained to this day with all its beauty.[7]

MODERN REINVENTION

Nicholas's medieval devotés added outlandish anec-
dotes to his biography, but he nonetheless retained his
essence, so to speak. In contrast, aside from kindness to
children and some stocking-stuffing, the modern Santa
Claus bears almost no resemblance to the saint whose
name he bears. The difference between the two is com-
parable to the difference between "development" and
"evolution." When a creature develops, it goes from
being an infant to an adult. When a creature evolves, it
goes from being a fish to a mammal.

The details of how this evolution came about are not
entirely clear except for the time and location: we know
that it took place in New York City around the early
nineteenth century. *Sinter Klaas* is the Dutch rendering
of "St. Nicholas." Holland had become a Protestant
nation, but nevertheless the Dutch, a seafaring people,
had a deep devotion to Nicholas as the patron of mari-
ners and did not want to give the sack-bearing saint the
sack; after all, his image was the figurehead on the prow
of every Dutch boat. And so when Dutch Calvinists tried
to suppress the memory of Nicholas, the most they could
do was obliterate the details of his popish biography; his
feast day and the customs surrounding his visit remained
the same.[8] It was this legacy that the Dutch brought with

them when they founded New Amsterdam or what would become New York City.

The English who commandeered the city in 1664 were initially leery of Sinter Klaas because of his lingering ties to the Catholic cult of saints. On the other hand, the kindly Dutch figure *was* more appealing than their own "Father Christmas"—a personification of Christmas who was friendly, bearded, and fur-clad, but prior to his twentieth-century merger with the American Santa Claus had no association with gifts or children. It was a point in favor of Sinter Klaas that English children—and who can blame them?—very much liked a tradition of receiving gifts every year from a miraculous visitor.[9]

Thanks to the American melting pot, a compromise was struck: the exchange of gifts would be moved from the fifth of December to the twenty-fifth, and so many elements would be added to the story of the annual gift-giver that he would no longer be recognizable as a saintly Catholic bishop. Contributors to the new Santa Claus included poets like Washington Irving, who portrayed Santa flying in a wagon in 1809; the 1821 anonymous poem "The Children's Friend," which portrays a wagon pulled by a solitary reindeer, and Clement Clarke Moore's poem "The Night Before Christmas" (published in 1823), which has been described as "arguably the best-known verses ever written by an American."[10] Moore added much to the Santa Claus legend, including the now canonical depiction of him driving a sleigh with eight named reindeer.

The American poets borrowed several features from Father Christmas but added their own touches, portraying Santa Claus as married, pipe-smoking, jolly and portly, clad in fur and whiskered in white. But there is one interesting difference between their picture of him and ours today; they thought of him not as the great employer of elves but as "a right jolly old elf"

Santa Claus, drafted into service for the Union cause by Thomas Nast. *Harper's Weekly*

himself. The early accounts portray Santa as diminutive, with a "miniature sleigh," as Moore wrote it, and "eight tiny reindeer." Even the familiar depictions of cartoonist Thomas Nast from the 1860s are of a dwarf-sized character. It would not be until the end of the nineteenth century that Santa achieved full-sized, human stature.

Other factors fueled Santa's evolution. Nast's use of Santa Claus to support the cause of the Union North did much to bolster the gift-giver's celebrity, and it was soon answered by the South with Louise Clack's 1867 *General Lee and Santa Claus*. The success of Charles Dickens in

From the March 19, 1870, *Illustrated London News* story on "Dickens's Farewell Reading." *Charles Dickens Museum*

making Christmas warmer and fuzzier helped set the conditions for Santa's popularity, even though he does not appear in any of Dickens's stories. Finally, it would be difficult to underestimate the influence of commercialism, with merchants and manufacturers heartily embracing the Santa Claus myth to ratchet up sales. One particularly successful example is from Coca-Cola in the 1930s; their ads featuring Haddon Sundblom's illustrations of a rosy-cheeked Santa enjoying a coke have become iconic. It didn't hurt that Santa's red-and-white outfit had the same colors as the soft drink brand.

But besides the borrowings from Father Christmas, from where did Washington Irving and his peers obtain their strange details about Santa Claus? According to one intriguing theory, the answer is the god of Norse and Germanic mythology after whom Thursday is named: Thor.[11] Consider the similarities: Thor was a large, jovial, bearded old man whose symbolic color was red (owing to his association with fire). Thunder was said to have been caused by the rolling of his chariot (drawn by two white goats) across the clouds, and his home was said to have been "Northland," somewhere among the icebergs. The fireplace was considered sacred to Thor because it was through it that he came into his element, the fire.[12]

Still another theory is that Odin or Woden (after whom Wednesday is named) is the main inspiration, for he is portrayed as a god with a long white beard who distributes gifts during Yuletide astride Sleipnir, his flying eight-footed horse.[13] If either theory is correct and Santa's creators were consciously or unconsciously drawing from mythology, then the change from St. Nicholas to Santa Claus is not the product of evolution after all; it is the metamorphosis of a Christian saint into an amalgamated pagan god. That's quite a leap, even for Santa's reindeer!

On the other hand, the stories about Thor and Woden may themselves be reconstructions and perhaps even inventions of nineteenth-century anthropologists and folklorists. That, at least, is the accusation of scholars such as Charles W. Jones, author of *Saint Nicholas of Myra, Bari, and Manhattan*, who calls the supposed mythological origin of Santa Claus' features "a legend of a legend."[14] And so the debate continues.

EXTREME MAKEOVER AND LASTING VALUE

America has always been a great place to become a self-made man, but it's possible to imagine that St.

Nicholas might be a bit confused by the way that America has remade him. Phyllis McGinley has a hilarious poem about the transformation of this popular saint. "He who had feared the world's applause," she observes, "Now, with a beard, is Santa Claus." While this "multiplied elf" goes around spinning yarns and increasing sales, the saint who passed away in the odor of sanctity now dizzily "spins in his grave."[15]

Phyllis McGinley, a devout Catholic, also published two stories that developed the Santa Claus myth further: *The Year Without a Santa Claus* (1956) and *How Mrs. Santa Claus Saved Christmas* (1963). Cynics may accuse McGinley of hypocrisy, but I suspect her writings have a deeper consistency: have fun with the Santa Claus fairy tale, but don't forget the holy man behind it. At the very least, don't forget the *holiness* behind it. G. K. Chesterton, whose belly also shook like a bowl full of jelly, testified to the value that even a secular Santa brings to the table. His reflections are worth quoting at length.

> What has happened to me has been the very reverse of what appears to be the experience of most of my friends. Instead of dwindling to a point, Santa Claus has grown larger and larger in my life until he fills almost the whole of it. It happened in this way. As a child I was faced with a phenomenon requiring explanation; I hung up at the end

of my bed an empty stocking, which in the morning became a full stocking. I had done nothing to produce the things that filled it. I had not worked for them, or made them, or helped to make them. I had not even been good—far from it. And the explanation was that a certain being whom people called Santa Claus was benevolently disposed towards me. Of course, most people who talk

Christmas morning. *Kaufmann & Strauss Co.*

about these things get into a state of some mental confusion by attaching tremendous importance to the name of the entity. We called him Santa Claus, because everyone called him Santa Claus; but the name of a god is a mere human label. His real name may have been Williams. It may have been the Archangel Uriel. What we believed was that a certain benevolent agency did give us those toys for nothing. And, as I say, I believe it still. I have merely extended the idea. Then I only wondered who put the toys in the stocking; now I wonder who put the stocking by the bed, and the bed in the room, and the room in the house, and the house on the planet, and the great planet in the void. Once I only thanked Santa Claus for a few dolls and crackers, now I thank him for stars and street faces and wine and the great sea. Once I thought it delightful and astonishing to find a present so big that it only went halfway into the stocking. Now I am delighted and astonished every morning to find a present so big that it takes two stockings to hold it, and then leaves a great deal outside; it is the large and preposterous present of myself, as to the origin of which I can afford no suggestion except that Santa Claus gave it to me in a fit of peculiarly fantastic goodwill.[16]

Chapter Five

THE GOOD, THE BAD, AND THE UGLY: SANTA'S HELPERS

S
ince giving gifts to the entire world on a single night is a fairly big job, St. Nicholas and Santa Claus do not work alone. Let us start with St. Nick, who has the larger variety of helpers, and conclude with Santa's elves and reindeer.

COMPANIONS OF ST. NICHOLAS

ANIMALS

Before there were eight flying reindeer, St. Nicholas had more domestic help from the barnyard. In France, Belgium, and other countries, the Bishop of Myra uses a gift-laden donkey. It would appear that before the Reformation, he used a Yule Goat in Scandinavia (see "Christmas Gnome and Yule Goat" in the next chapter for interesting developments in that story since the Reformation). In the Netherlands, as we have seen, Nicholas has a trusty white steed named Schimmel and Dutch boys and girls leave out carrots or hay for him on St. Nicholas's Eve. The custom of feeding Sinter Klaas's horse allegedly comes from a pre-Christian practice in which children filled their boots with carrots and hay and placed them near the chimney to feed the Norse god Woden's flying eight-footed horse Sleipnir; when Woden (a.k.a. Odin) flew by, he would reward them with gifts.

BERCHTA

In some parts of Germany and Austria, St. Nick is assisted by a female figure named Berchta (a.k.a. Bertha, Berchtel, Budelfrau, Buzebergt, or Perchta). Derived from the goddess wife of Woden, and drafted into assisting at the celebration of Christ's birth, she can either be friendly or terrifying, a bringer of gifts to children who know their prayers or the leader of the "Wild Hunt," a procession of damned souls and wicked spirits across the night sky. Berchtel "used to punish the naughty children with a rod, and reward the good with nuts and apples; Buzebergt wore black rags, had her face blackened and her hair hanging unkempt, and carried a pot of starch which she smeared upon people's faces."[1]

BLACK PETE

In the Netherlands, *Pieten* are the stately bishop's fun-loving and mischievous servants who distribute treats after St. Nicholas has interrogated the children about their catechism or behavior. The most famous (and politically incorrect) of these is Zwarte Piet or Black Pete, a Moor who appears in blackface and royal servant's clothes.

The Dutch Sinterklaas and Zwarte Piet. *Courtesy of Michell Zappa*[1]

CERT

Cert (the Czech name for the Devil) is a companion-demon in in the Czech Republic and Slovakia. Cert is enchained and chaperoned by a good angel dressed in white to make sure he does not harm the children. Cert often carries a whip or a staff or chains to warn children of the wages of naughtiness; he also gives bad children coal or potatoes and sports a sack for carrying really bad children off to Hell.

HANS TRAPP

In Alsace-Lorraine, Hans Trapp is a wealthy and ruthless man who was excommunicated by the Church, sold his soul to the Devil, and went into exile in the forests, where he disguised himself as a scarecrow in order to capture and eat children. After being struck by God with a bolt of lightning, Hans now atones for his misdeeds at the side of St. Nicholas, admonishing naughty children not to be like him. Hans Trapp holds a unique position among St. Nicholas's wicked companions, for he is the only one based on a real human being. Hans von Trotha was a tall and arrogant fifteenth-century knight from the region who flooded an entire town out of spite and was excommunicated by the Church. After his death, his malicious behavior and imposing appearance became the grist of local lore.

HOLY HELPMATES

Since around the sixteenth century, St. Nicholas has also counted on a motley assortment of holy assistants. At the upper end of the spectrum, the munificent bishop enjoyed the cooperation of one or more angels, St. Peter, and sometimes, even the Christ Child Himself (see Chapter Six). In Tyrol, Austria, St. Nicholas used to split his duties with another popular saint: boys received gifts on his feast on December 6 while St. Lucy gave gifts to girls on her feast day on December 13. It is from this same tradition in Switzerland, incidentally, that Mrs. Claus gets her first name there: Lucy.[3]

HOUSEKER

In Luxembourg, Houseker or Hoesecker is a long-haired, soot-faced ruffian dressed in a long brown robe and carrying a chain that he uses to announce St. Nicholas. Like a number of other of the saint's sidekicks, Houseker punishes naughty children with his switch and threatens to carry them off in his sack.

KNECHT RUPRECHT

In northern Germany, Knecht Ruprecht or Servant Rupert is either a farmhand or a wild foundling raised by Nicholas, but since "Rupert" or "Robert" is a German nickname for the Devil, there is also a hint of the sinister. Dressed like Houseker, Rupert asks children if they know their prayers and either rewards them with treats or hits them with his bag of ashes.

KRAMPUS

Rupert is tame in comparison with Krampus, a terrifying half-goat, half-demon found in southern Austria, southern Germany, and outlying areas (in Tyrol, Austria, he is known as Klaubauf). Horned and furry with a long red tongue, he is armed with a rod or whip for punishing naughty children and wears a wooden basket for abducting them; kindly St. Nicholas, however, always prevents him from carrying out his plan. And to show that the saint is in control, Krampus usually appears in chains, which he rattles violently to great effect. In some areas, Krampus or even groups of Krampuses roam the streets causing mayhem on *Krampusnacht*, the night of December 5.

MUTANT NICHOLASES

The Reformation was not kind to the saints, even to the ones who brought gifts. In England, Nicholas's memory survived only in the custom of the Boy Bishop. In the Protestant areas of Central Europe, Nicholas survived mostly in secular and reduced distortions. Ru-Klaus or Rough Nicholas has a rugged appearance, Aschenklas or Ashy Nicholas carries a bag of ashes, and Pelznickel or Furry Nicholas is clad in fur; all of them bring gifts for the nice and switches for the naughty. In the United States the Pennsylvania Dutch held on to Pelznickel in the form of Belsnickel. You may remember his 2012 appearance in episode nine, season nine of *The Office*, "Dwight Christmas."

And as folk customs are not renowned for their consistency, these deformed versions of Nicholas sometimes later became *companions* of St. Nicholas or the Christ Child (see below). We conjecture that because sweet Baby Jesus is not an ideal candidate for carrying out the punishment of the disobedient, the mutant Nicholases were allowed to do the dirty work.

PÈRE FOUETTARD

In France and Luxembourg, St. Nicholas is accompanied by the murderous innkeeper who pickled the three boys (see Chapter Four). Père Fouettard or "Father Whipping,"[4] as he is now called, gives out lumps of coal and beatings to the naughty while Nicholas distributes gifts to the nice.

SCHMUTZLI

In Switzerland, the soot-faced Schmutzli bears a faint resemblance to Hans Trapp, even though he has pre-Christian origins. The menacing figure attacks children with his broom of twigs and threatens to stuff them in his sack and carry them off to the woods to be eaten if they are bad.

TOO CREEPY?

The St. Nicholas Center, which has the admirable goal of educating "people of faith and the wider public about the true St. Nicholas," is not happy with the figures mentioned in this chapter. We do not "wish to perpetuate in any way customs that include characters with a dark side," they declare. "We abhor the imagery of these characters."[5]

Such a reaction is understandable, but maybe they should have a little sympathy for the Devil. There is a point to these spooky sidekicks. Culturally, they capture pre-Christian Yuletide practices and convert them to Christian use. Psychologically, they release the almost universal primordial fear of a kidnapping bogeyman, who is often portrayed carrying a sack. Biographically, they recall the many demons that Nicholas exorcized from the pagan groves and temples of Myra (hey, perhaps he kept one as a permanent POW). Narratively, they add drama to the evening and serve as a perfect foil for the kindly saint. Morally, they highlight the importance of piety and ethical behavior and the fact that actions have consequences. Theologically, they illustrate the need for intercessors such as St. Nicholas and demonstrate how Almighty God, even though He does not author evil, can make it serve His purposes. (And, as we will see in Chapter Seven, there are yet other reasons that Christmas has a dark side). At the very least, St. Nick's unsavory associates keep the season from degenerating into pure sentimentality.

TEAM SANTA CLAUS

St. Nicholas's companions may be colorful, but they are outnumbered by the vast team working for Santa. In addition to the ever-faithful Mrs. Claus, Santa relies on flying reindeer and an army of elves at the North Pole.

REINDEER

Santa Claus is first mentioned as having a single flying reindeer in an anonymous 1821 poem entitled "Old Santeclaus with Much Delight." Two years later Clement Clark Moore's poem "A Visit from St. Nicholas" (better known as "The Night Before Christmas") introduced "eight tiny reindeer" by their names: Dasher, Dancer, Prancer, Vixen, Comet, Cupid, Donner, and Blitzen. We do not know why Moore chose these names or the number eight, although one theory is that they were inspired by the god Woden's eight-footed flying steed Sleipnir. Similarly, the original idea for a flying reindeer pulling a sleigh may have come from Thor's chariot pulled by two flying goats, which travel across the sky and make thunder when they roll over the clouds.

In 1939, thanks to the success of a Montgomery Ward department store children's book written by Robert L. May, a ninth reindeer was added: Rudolph the red-nosed reindeer. For the story behind this famous song, see Chapter Nine.

Santa plotting his trip on a globe. *Saturday Evening Post*

ELVES

To us, who have grown up with images of Christmas elves in green outfits with pointy ears and even pointier hats working in Santa's Workshop, it is surprising to learn that in old European mythology, elves were scary, mischievous creatures who could be helpful when bribed but were dangerous when slighted, something all too easy to do, especially around this time of year.[6] Christians were suspicious of the little critters: the early English poem *Beowulf* links ogres and elves and evil phantoms with the curse of Cain (lines 111–12). But elves took a more benign turn in the early nineteenth century. In Moore's 1823 poem "The Night Before Christmas,"

Rockwell's iconic painting of Santa and his elves. *Saturday Evening Post*

the only elf that is mentioned is Santa Claus himself, who now is not a Catholic saint or even a full-sized human being but a plump "right jolly old elf." One of the first times that elves are mentioned helping Santa is an 1859 poem entitled "The Wonders of Santa Claus":

In his house upon the top of a hill,
And almost out of sight,
He keeps a great many elves at work,
All working with all their might,
To make a million of pretty things,
Cakes, sugar-plums, and toys,
To fill the stockings, hung up you know
By the little girls and boys.[7]

Over the next fifty years, Santa Claus grew to human stature and was surrounded by innocent and industrious elves. Normal Rockwell's 1922 iconic painting *Santa with Elves* cemented this image, which remains with us today.

Chapter Six

SANTA'S COMPETITION: OTHER GIFT-GIVERS

St. Nicholas has never had a monopoly on gift-giving. In this chapter we look at some of Santa's competitors.

BABBO NATALE

Babbo Natale means "Daddy Christmas" in Italian— essentially Santa Claus by another name. In some areas of Italy he replaces Befana (see below) as the principal gift-giver, but on Christmas Eve rather than Epiphany Eve.

BABOUSHKA

Because Babushka or Baboushka (Russian for "grandmother") kept the tidiest house in town, the

Magi asked if they could stay the night with her. The next morning, they invited her to join them on their journey to worship the newborn King. According to one version of the story, she said no in order to tidy up first; according to another, she not only refused but gave the Three Kings the wrong directions (fortunately they were wise enough to figure it out). Either way, Baboushka regretted her decision and has been seeking the Infant Jesus ever since. In Russia she used to give gifts to children in their rooms on Epiphany Eve, but the Communists were not kind to Baboushka, and she is hardly known to most Russians today.

BASIL, SAINT

Basil the Great (330–379) was a bishop of Caesarea and an eloquent Father and Doctor of the Church who defended the divinity of the Holy Spirit from heretical naysayers; he also founded Eastern monasticism. None of these achievements makes Basil particularly well-suited to giving presents and treats, but there is one story about him that does. The Roman prefect of Cappadocia had demanded an exorbitant tax from the population, and so the people sadly gathered their valuables to give to him. St. Basil, however, appealed to the prefect and had the tax repealed. Since the people could not be sure whose valuables among the collection were whose, Basil advised them to make small pies. The saint then put the valuables into the pies, and each person miraculously received what was originally his. It is this legend that inspires the Greek *Vasilopita* or St. Basil cake, which has a coin hidden in it (see Chapter Twelve).

And there is another reason for Basil's association with gift-giving. The saint died on January 1, and his feast is kept on that day by the Greek Orthodox Church. And since January 1 is a traditional Greco-Roman day for exchanging gifts, in Greece Basil has assumed the role reserved in other places for St. Nicholas or Santa Claus. On New Year's Eve (or sometimes New Year's Day), the holy bishop visits Greek homes and leaves presents in a corner, on the holiday table, or under the Christmas tree if there is one.

BEFANA

Befana or Bufana (a corruption of *Epiphania*), has a biography similar to that of Russia's Baboushka. Befana was asked by the Magi to join them on their journey to Bethlehem, but she delayed so she could put her house in order (she was an excellent housekeeper) and missed her opportunity to see the Christ Child. Ever since she has been looking for Him. Another version has Befana being rude to the Holy Family on their flight to Egypt, and still another has Befana suffering from the loss of her own child. Mad with grief, she thought that Jesus was her son and gave Him gifts. Moved with compassion, the Christ Child rewarded Befana by making her the mother of every child in Italy.

Today, Befana is a sort of fairy godmother figure who rides a broomstick through the air. She is an old hag dressed in a black shawl and covered in soot (because of all her visits down the chimney), but she is usually smiling and always carrying a bag or hamper filled with treats. If you see Befana flying through the air, however, she will whack you with her broom, as she prefers to perform her ministry in secret (this last detail is no doubt designed to keep the little ones in bed). Befana gives gifts to children on Epiphany Eve, but she may also leave a coal, a stick, or a bag of ashes for the naughty. She may even sweep the floor for you before she leaves.

BERCHTA

We met Berchta (a.k.a. Bertha, Berchtel, Budelfrau, Buzebergt, Perchta, or Frau Holle) in the previous chapter—the curious figure who is said to be derived from the goddess wife of Odin (a.k.a. Woden) and conscripted into assisting at the celebration of Christ's birth. Whatever her origins, she is a mixed bag. As we have seen, in some German-speaking areas she is a terrifying figure who leads the terrifying "Wild Hunt." But in others, she is a kindly old woman who rocks children to sleep, hears children recite their prayers, and rewards them with treats. Like Befana, Berchta is associated with Epiphany and often gives gifts on the vigil of the feast.

THE CHRIST CHILD

Although Martin Luther initially kept the Feast of St. Nicholas and bought children presents for the occasion, he later condemned the practice as idolatrous and moved the gift-giving to Christmas Day under the auspices of the Christ Child or Kristkindl.[1] The Christ Child, who is occasionally portrayed by a blond-haired girl, became the principal gift-giver in certain parts of Germany, Austria, and France in both Protestant and Catholic areas; in fact, in Germany today, it is only Catholic areas that still observe this custom. What would Luther say upon learning that only Catholics and not Lutherans are keeping his custom?

In Spain and Spanish-speaking countries, the manger is empty for nine days before Christmas. Children write notes to Baby Jesus and place them in front of the empty crib; angels then come and carry the requests to Heaven. Then, on Christmas morning, the Child Jesus (*el Niño Jesús*) is found in the crib surrounded by the presents He has brought.

Oddly, in America, the word *Kristkindl* inspired a new name for *Santa Claus*: "Kris Kringle." So Jesus became Santa Claus, who was once St. Nicholas, who worshipped Jesus. Got it.

Another remarkable transformation took place in Louisiana's Cajun country, when the Kristkindl brought by Swiss immigrants became "La Christine," a woman who brings homemade treats and small gifts on New Year's Eve.

CHRISTMAS GNOME AND YULE GOAT

It is perhaps ironic that some of the nations closest to the North Pole show little interest in Santa Claus but turn instead to Yule Gnomes (*Jultomten* in Swedish, *Juleman-den* or *Julenissen* in Danish, and *Julenissen* in Norwegian). Originally, countries like Sweden probably had St. Nicholas bring them presents with the help of a Yule Goat (*Julbock*), but after the Reformation, St. Nicholas was kicked out and the Yule Goat became the principal gift-giver. With the rise of the American Santa Claus in the nineteenth century (who, remember, was originally an elf), the Swedes and others countered with their native gnomes and made the Yule Goat their pack animal. Today a Christmas gnome, who closely resembles a garden gnome in appearance, and a Christmas goat travel from house to house distributing presents. Inside, a bowl of porridge awaits the gnome to thank him for his generosity.

As for the goat, he is honored in other ways. Since 1966 the town of Gävle, Sweden, has erected a Guinness World

The Gävle Goat in 2004. *Courtesy of Baltica*[1]

Records–winning Yule Goat made entirely out of straw. The towering effigy, which stands in the town square, is built by volunteers at the beginning of Advent. Although the townspeople are proud of their goat, it has a way of bringing out the vandal in people. Despite fencing, security cameras, guards, and flame-retardants, the Gävle Goat has been damaged or destroyed thirty-seven times between 1966 and 2020. Methods include kicking it to pieces, stealing it, and hitting it with a car, but the most popular means of destruction is arson. In 2005, for example, hooligans dressed like Santa Claus and the Gingerbread Man torched the goat by shooting a flaming arrow at it.

FATHER CHRISTMAS

An English personification of Christmas at least as old as the sixteenth century, Father Christmas came to be portrayed as an old man with a long white beard, a full-length robe, and a pointed hood. Initially he was thin as well, but by the late eighteenth century he had grown fat and wore holly in his hair. Father Christmas and other holiday customs fell into disuse in England under the reign of the Stuarts, but Ben Jonson wrote a play in which the old man pleads for his return: "Why, I am no dangerous person, and so I told my friends o' the guard. I am old Gregory Christmas still, and though I come out of the Pope's Head Alley, as good a Protestant as any i' my parish."[3]

Scrooge's nephew and his friends play blind man's buff. *Charles Green*

For the first four centuries of his existence, Father Christmas was not a gift-giver to children but a patron of adult feasting and drinking, an embodiment of Christmas merriment. After the rise of Santa Claus, however, Father Christmas felt the need to change his image, and so in the nineteenth century he, too, turned his attention to the little ones.

GRANDFATHER FROST

Ded Moroz, or Grandfather Frost, was a pre-Christian personification of winter in Russia. Initially, the Bolsheviks who founded the Soviet Union rejected Grandfather Frost and all other magical gift-givers (such as St. Nicholas, Baboushka, and Kolyáda), but eventually, under Josef Stalin in the 1940s, they decided to give Grandfather Frost a secular makeover and double down on him. Grandfather Frost was only to give gifts on New Year's Eve (a civic rather than religious holiday). Attired in a new ankle-length blue fur coat and a round fur hat, he has a long white beard and carries a long magical staff. Grandfather Frost is accompanied by his niece or granddaughter the Snow Maiden, and both protect the children's gifts from the thieving witch Baba Yaga (whom we will meet in Chapter Seven). Grandfather Frost remains popular in contemporary Russia and some parts of the old Soviet bloc, although some former satellite states such as Ukraine view Grandfather Frost as a bitter reminder of Communist oppression.

JOULUPUKKI

Finland's version of Santa Claus is literally named "Yule Goat." One theory is that the Yule Goat was a pagan tradition of a man turned into a goat-man or a man in goatskins. (To this day, in some parts of Finland, people impersonate goats and put on a performance in exchange for food.) But the Finnish Joulupukki, like the Yule Goat who now accompanies the Christmas Gnome in Sweden, may have developed from St. Nicholas's pack animal after the saint himself was banned by Protestant Reformers. Whatever the provenance, radio broadcasts in the 1920s helped merge the Yule Goat with Santa Claus. Perhaps it was an easy transition: after all, the Finns actually have reindeer in their country.

KOLYÁDA

Kolyáda is named after the season she claims as her own; her name is derived from the name for a pre-Christian Slavic and Baltic winter festival. The figure Kolyáda is a white-robed maiden driven about in a sleigh from house to house on Christmas Eve. In order to receive presents, youngsters sing carols to her, carols such as this:

> Kolyáda! Kolyáda!
> Kolyáda has arrived
> On the Eve of the Nativity.
> We went about, we sought
> Holy Kolyáda,
> Through all the courts, in all the alleys.
> We found Kolyáda
> In Peter's Court.
> Round Peter's Court there is an iron fence,
> In the midst of the Court there are three rooms:
> In the first room is the bright Moon;
> In the second room, the red Sun;
> And in the third room, the many Stars.[4]

Kolyáda is probably a Christianized makeover of an ancient sun goddess who took her seat in her cart after the winter solstice and urged her horses onto the summer track. Before the rise of the Soviet Communists (who replaced her with the Snow Maiden who accompanies Grandfather Frost), she was a popular gift-giver in Belarus, Ukraine, and some parts of Russia. Now, alas, the poor dear is all but forgotten.

ST. LUCY

We have already described some of the charming customs of St. Lucy's Day in Chapter Two, but here are a couple more. In Chapter Five we saw how St. Nicholas gives presents to boys on the eve of his December 6 feast day while St. Lucy gives presents to girls on the eve of her December 13 feast day in parts of Austria and Switzerland. In her native Sicily and other parts of Italy, St. Lucy brings presents to both boys and girls. On the vigil of her feast, hay is put outside the door for her donkey while a treat is placed on the table inside for the visiting saint.

ST. MARTIN

St. Martin's Day on November 11 used to be a great feast day with feasting, parades, plays, and more. And because Martin of Tours (316–397) is renowned for giving half his cloak to a beggar shivering in the cold (who turned out to be Jesus Christ), it is fitting that the saintly bishop should be assigned the task of distributing gifts. In Nuremberg, Germany, and the surrounding areas, children put their boots near the front door on St. Martin's Eve, and the next morning they are miraculously filled with sweets.

THE MAGI

Perhaps the most logical arrangement of all is having the Wise Men bring gifts for the holidays: if they did it once, they can do it again. In Spanish-speaking countries, while the Infant Jesus (*el Niño Jesús*) bestows presents on Christmas Day, the Three Kings (*los Tres Reges Magos*) take over on their feast day. Children write letters to the Magi requesting gifts and leave out drinks for the Magi and food for their camels on Epiphany Eve. Then the Wise Men visit their homes while they are asleep and deposit little gifts in the children's shoes. After the children attend Mass the next morning, they can have the gifts. The Magi often leave presents for the grown-ups as well. These customs remain popular in Latin America, although the American Santa Claus has been gaining ground. Consequently, several Catholic bishops have preached against the right jolly old elf as an invasive non-native species.

PÈRE NOËL

Centuries ago many French children received gifts from the Christ Child (*le Petit Jésus* or *le Petit Noël*), but today Père Noël ("Father Christmas") does most of the work. This personification of Christmas bears a close resemblance to England's Father Christmas in attire and origin, but he also shares some qualities with St. Nicholas and Santa Claus. On Christmas Eve children leave their shoes by the fireplace and carrots for Père Noël's donkey, Gui (French for "mistletoe"). They also leave a treat for Gui's owner, but since most French adults would laugh at the idea of drinking milk, it is usually a glass of wine or Calvados. Whatever the potation, Père Noël repays the kindness by coming down the chimney and giving the children gifts. Traditionally, these gifts were only those that were small enough to fit in their shoes (candy, small toys, coins, and so forth), but nowadays he also leaves larger gifts under the tree. Sometimes the kindly man borrows a sidekick from St. Nicholas and is accompanied by that scourge of the naughty known as Père Fouettard, the murderous innkeeper figure we met in Chapter Five.

In Louisiana's Cajun country, "Papa Noël" arrives in a pirogue (a flat-bottomed boat used in the bayou) pulled by eight alligators. One of them, Nicolette, has glowing green eyes that guide the team through the dark swamps.

TANTE ARIE

In the Franche-Comté region of France and the canton of Jura, Switzerland, a kindly old fairy named Tante Arie ("Aunt Arie") comes down from her mountain home on Christmas Eve with her donkey, Marion. Sometimes she disguises herself and asks for hospitality in order to get to know the inhabitants and their habits. Tante Arie gives presents to good children and dunce caps or switches to naughty ones. According to legend, she is the reincarnation of Countess Henriette de Montbéliard (1387–1444), a ruler of the region who was renowned for her kindness and generosity.

WEIHNACHTSMANN

Weihnachtsmann ("Christmas Man") is the German version of Santa Claus. He differs only slightly from his American counterpart. Instead of eight reindeer, he rides a white horse like St. Nicholas, and he does not deign to slide down chimneys. His timing is slightly different as well: the "big reveal" of presents takes place after Christmas Eve dinner rather than Christmas morning. A nationwide survey in 1932 revealed that half of German children awaited Weihnachtsmann to bring them presents while the other half awaited Kristkindl, but today Christmas Man has edged out the Christ Child except in the traditionally Catholic areas of Germany.[5]

YULE LADS

In Iceland, the Yule Lads (*Jólasveinar*) were originally terrifying creatures, goblins born of the child-eating ogres Gryla and Leppaludi. Thankfully, although Iceland remains justifiably proud of her folkloric tradition, the tiny island nation lightened up in the nineteenth century and followed the trend of domesticating Christmas and making it more child-friendly. The Yule Lads were duly transformed. Today there are thirteen of them, who descend one by one from their mountain home in Iceland's interior, beginning on St. Lucy's Eve (December 12) and ending on Christmas Eve (December 24). Each has his own name and is distinguished by a favorite prank he likes to play. During the Twelve Days of Christmas, the Lads depart one by one in the same way, until they are all gone by Epiphany.

In the days leading up to Christmas, children leave their shoes out for the Yule Lads to fill with small treats. Naughty children receive a rotten piece of fruit or a potato.

Chapter Seven

COME TO THE DARK SIDE: CHRISTMAS AND THE GHOULS

*There'll be scary ghost stories
And tales of the glories of
Christmases long, long ago.*

—EDWARD POLA AND GEORGE WYLE, "It's the Most
Wonderful Time of the Year"

"It's the Most Wonderful Time of the Year" is a rather vapid 1963 song extolling the virtues of a modern secular Christmas. Why does it list the telling of scary ghost stories as a standard Christmas activity? The answer is that only recently has Christmas become the sentimental stuff of sugar plums dancing in our heads. The

Illustration for *The Haunted Man and the Ghost's Bargain*, a Christmas ghost story by Charles Dickens. *Fred Barnes*

Christmas story itself involves fear, uncertainty, and death: after a stressful night seeking lodging for a woman in labor, the Infant Jesus is born in a manger and hunted by Herod's murderous henchmen. And for our distant pagan forebears, winter was a dreadful season that involved a constant fight against the cold and a struggle to stay fed. When springtime finally came, the peoples of Europe held mock burials of winter, burning it in effigy and bidding it good riddance with wild abandon. (This custom, by the way, continued in some places into the twentieth century.)

Not surprisingly, then, pre-Christian European mythology portrayed winter, when the nights were long and everything except the mysterious mistletoe and some evergreens seemed dead, as a time when evil prevailed. Demons were said to be active at the approach of the winter solstice, and when the days began to grow longer, they fought vehemently against the increase of light. "It was a time," writes Francis X. Weiser, "when all the evil spirits freely roamed the world, when the souls of the dead returned to haunt the humans, when the giants of snow, ice, and storm endeavored to extinguish the growing flame of light and life in nature."[1]

Perhaps our ancestors were onto something, in a bizarre way. Yuletide devils are real. Besides the weather-related hardships of winter, there are the psychological effects of the season: seasonal affective disorder, stress, depression, suicide, alcohol abuse, family strife, and so forth. The Swiss even have a name for the Christmas blues: *Weihnachtscholer*. (Psychologists, on the other hand, call it Post-Christmas Traumatic Syndrome). One way to think about the old spooky elements of Christmas is that they are a subliminal way of addressing and coping with these issues.

And here is another consideration: the dark side of Christmas, like the shadows in the principle of chiaroscuro in art, makes the lights of Christmas that much brighter. We define coziness as "comfort in the midst of discomfort." The couple hanging out on a warm tropical beach in a Corona beer commercial are clearly enjoying the moment, but they are not cozy. Christmas coziness is one of the greatest feelings on earth, but it requires the presence of a real threat. It is only when the weather outside is frightful that the fire is so delightful.

So let us look at the dark side of Christmas—and the strange figures who represent it—with a renewed spirit of appreciation.

BABA YAGA

"Witchy Old Woman," or Baba Yaga, is a strikingly ambiguous figure from Slavic folklore who sometimes helps people and sometimes eats children. As we saw in the last chapter, she plays a minor role in the Grandfather Frost legend, serving as a foil who wants to steal children's presents.

BERCHTA

Berchta can also be strikingly ambiguous, as we saw in Chapters Five and Six. In some regions she is naughty, in some nice, and in some both. In several German-speaking areas she leads wicked spirits and damned souls across the night sky in a procession called the "Wild Hunt" (Johnny Cash's "Ghost Riders in the Sky" is based on this legend). In Bavaria and Austria, she roams the countryside during the Twelve Days of Christmas and is especially active on the vigil of "her" feast, Epiphany. It is then that she enters homes and inquires into the behavior of children and servants. If they have worked hard all year, they might find a silver coin in their shoes or in a bucket; if they have not, Berchta will disembowel them and replace their innards with straw.

BOGEYMEN

Among mankind's most primal fears is the dread of being abducted (especially as a child) and of being a victim of cannibalism. Early fairy tales, before they were

Disneyized, are rife with these eerie themes: think Hansel and Gretel. As we saw in Chapter Five, Christmas confronts these fears with St. Nicholas's wicked assistants, whose job it is to punish naughty children. In France, as we saw in Chapters Five and Six, the innkeeper Père Fouettard murdered and pickled three boys, presumably to eat them later. In Alsace-Lorraine, Hans Trapp lives in the forest and disguises himself as a scarecrow in order to capture and eat children. The soot-faced Schmutzli in Switzerland is a menacing figure with pre-Christian origins who attacks children with his broom of twigs and threatens to stuff them in his sack and carry them off to the woods to be eaten if they are bad.

CHRISTMAS CAT?

One of the more peculiar baddies of the Christmas season may be found in Icelandic folklore. The Christmas Cat (a.k.a. Yule Cat) is a pet of the ogre Gryla, and he will eat anyone who does not get some new clothing for Christmas. The intention behind this menacing legend was to encourage hard work and cooperation among the womenfolk who made the clothes for the family as well as to incentivize children to behave well, for if they were denied new clothes on account of being naughty, they would get gobbled up. (It also reminded them not to mope if they only got socks for Christmas). Finally, the legend is a reminder to clothe the poor during winter—lest they become catnip.

THE CROSS AT THE CRIB

As we will see in Chapter Eight, some Christmas symbols point ahead to Jesus' Passion—holly, for example, which "bears a prickle, as sharp as any thorn." Why such macabre thoughts during such a joyous season? Well, the joy over Christ's Nativity springs from the fact that He is the One who will save us by His Passion, Death, and Resurrection.

Moreover, foreshadowing of the Crucifixion is built into the very narrative of Christmas. The warm cuddly images of the Gospel accounts of Christ's infancy contain hints of His future self-offering. Jesus is born in Bethlehem, which literally means "house of bread," and is laid in a "manger," which comes from a word to eat. The reader is supposed to recognize that this babe is the Bread of Life: "if any man eat of this bread," Christ later explains, "he shall live for ever; and the bread that I will give, is my flesh, for the life of the world" (John 6:52). Jesus is wrapped in swaddling clothes, which are not a fuzzy onesie but a foreshadowing of his burial shroud. Finally, the Magi give Jesus gold, frankincense, and myrrh: gold for His kingship, frankincense for His divinity, and myrrh for His death. The Epiphany carol "We Three Kings" contains the following explanation of the burial herb myrrh:

> Myrrh is mine; its bitter perfume
> Breathes a life of gathering gloom;—

Sorrowing, sighing, bleeding, dying,
Sealed in the stone-cold tomb.

DEVILS

To call the Babe in Bethlehem a Savior is to acknowl-edge a need for saving. But from whom or what? Christ-mastime devils remind us of the answer. As we saw in Chapter Five, St. Nicholas is sometimes accompanied by demons: Cert, Krampus, and Knecht Ruprecht (sort of).

The bells of some churches in the British Isles would toll mournfully, as if for a Requiem, one hour before midnight on Christmas Eve and then peal joyfully at the stroke of twelve. The funereal ringing was called "the Devil's funeral."

Devils can even be present by their absence. Shake-speare alludes to an old tradition when he has Marcellus declare in *Hamlet*:

> Some say that ever 'gainst that season comes
> Wherein our Saviour's birth is celebrated,
> The bird of dawning singeth all night long:
> And then, they say, no spirit dare stir
>   abroad;
> The nights are wholesome; then no planets
>   strike,
> No fairy takes, no witch has power to
>   charm,
> So hallow'd and so gracious is the time.[2]

Others were not so confident that the Christmas season was fiend-free. Some Norwegians used to believe that the old Norse gods made war on Christians on Christmas Eve, filling the night air with a clattering of hooves and wild shrieks and carrying off any hapless human being they could find. And since the Christian critique of pagan gods is that they are demons in disguise, you can imagine how welcome these Wild Hunts were.

Because of this demonic activity, the Advent and Christmas seasons were a favorite time to "sain." "Saining," derived from "signing," is an old English word for making the sign of the cross on a thing or person "for the purpose of exorcizing a demon, warding off the evil influences of witches, poison, etc."[3] In the Middle Ages and beyond, it took on quite a few different expressions. In Scandinavia, St. Lucy's name (which means "light") was written over the doors on her December 13 feast day in order to drive away demonic darkness. In some parts of Central Europe, St. Thomas's feast day on December 21 began the period of the "Rough Nights," when country folk would use grotesque masks or loud noises such as the cracking of whips and the ringing of bells to expel demons in preparation for Christmas, as we saw in Chapter Two, and other pious strategies included farmers and their sons' walking around their land with incense and holy water while the rest of the family recited the rosary.[4] In Austria, December 31 was sometimes called *Rauchnacht* or "Smoke Night," when the paterfamilias went through the house and barn purifying them with incense and holy water.[5]

Many saining customs gravitated around New Year's Eve and Day in the hopes of expelling evil or bad luck for the next twelve months. In rural Herefordshire, England, farmers burned a large globe made of hawthorn and mistletoe early New Year's morning in the field to cast out demons and ensure a good crop. The Scottish used to fumigate the house with juniper smoke on New Year's Day and drink water from a "ford over which the living carried the dead to burial." This water from the "dead and living ford" was also sprinkled on the beds.[6] Noise-making on New Year's Eve, which is now used to salute the new year, is derived from a pre-Christian custom of driving away demons (see Chapter Twelve for more details).

Epiphany was also a popular occasion for saining. Among the Greeks and Russians, the Blessing of the Waters on Epiphany drives away goblins and woodsprites (see "Goblins" below). In parts of France and Switzerland, youngsters would run wild through the streets on Twelfth Night with torches and noise-makers such as whips and bells to frighten away ghosts, sprites, and devils. Sometimes they knocked on the doors of homes as they passed by as a kind of exorcism. In

England, it was important to "wassail" fruit-bearing trees on Epiphany Eve. Men would surround a tree, greet it, and drink to its health. Sometimes the tree would be sprinkled with cider, beaten with a switch, or threatened.

ELVES

See Chapter Five.

FAIRIES

"No fairy takes," Prince Hamlet declares, during the Christmas season. Takes what? Before they were made pretty and friendlier during the Victorian period, fairies were potentially menacing creatures who had a reputation for stealing babies, substituting changelings, and abducting the elderly. They could also be responsible for birth defects and disease. That said, there are some good Christmas fairies such as Tante Arie (see Chapter Six).

GHOSTS

As we mentioned at the beginning of this chapter, winter was the season when ghosts roamed the earth, and generally speaking, that was not a good thing. Many of the expulsion practices of Christmas Eve, New Year's Eve, and Epiphany were directed against the souls of the dead as well as the demonic (see "Devils" above). The terrifying Wild Hunt also involved a parade of damned souls (see Chapter Five).

But sometimes, the ghosts needed help. On Childermas (December 28), the ghosts of unbaptized children howled in the wind for assistance; if you called out a Christian name you could "baptize" the soul and help it to Heaven.

And sometimes, the ghosts were welcome because they were the souls of one's loved ones. In some Scandinavian countries, master and servant alike once slept on the floor on fleshly strewn

The Ghost of Christmas Past shows Scrooge his younger self. *Sol Eytinge Jr.*

hay in imitation of the Christ Child but also to leave the beds available for one's dearly departed who visited during Christmastime. And the Greeks still have a custom that on St. Basil's Eve (December 31), some of the cake is reserved for absent loved ones (see Chapter Twelve).

But the most famous Christmas ghost story of all is, of course, Charles Dickens's *A Christmas Carol*, the full title of which is *A Christmas Carol. In Prose. Being a Ghost Story of Christmas* (1844). Miserly Ebenezer Scrooge is visited by the Ghosts of Christmas Past,

The doppelgänger in *The Haunted Man and the Ghost's Bargain*. Felix O. Darley

Present, and Yet to Come and is changed forever into a kind and generous man. Dickens was fascinated by fairy tales and nursery stories, for he believed that their purpose was to encourage moral conversion, and by creating a Christmas fairy tale (of ghosts), he was drawing from a long tradition of folklore. Dickens's fifth and final Christmas novella, by the way, is *The Haunted Man and the Ghost's Bargain* (1848). Professor Redlaw, who has difficulty forgiving and forgetting, is visited by his doppelgänger. The ghost offers him the gift of being able to forget the past and promises that Redlaw will be able to share this gift with whomever he wishes. Redlaw accepts, and the adventure begins.

GOBLINS

Before Dickens composed his breakout *Christmas Carol*, he wrote a short story called "The Christmas Goblins" featuring a crabby old sexton and gravedigger named Gabriel Grubb, who is digging a grave after dusk on Christmas Eve (that's two no-nos: working at night in a churchyard and working on Christmas Eve). "What man wanders among graves on such a night as this?" cries a goblin nearby. "Gabriel Grubb! Gabriel Grubb!" replies "a wild chorus of voices that seemed to fill the churchyard." Gabriel is then taken to Hell, where he sees images of respectable, hard-working, and happy people. He awakens the next morning an altered man, for "he had learned lessons of gentleness and good-nature by his strange adventures in the goblin's cavern."

As in *A Christmas Carol*, Dickens was drawing upon an older tradition of Yuletide spooks. Almost every nationality had wicked spirits that predated Christianity, and many of these old spirits were put in service of the Gospel. The pint-sized fiends were quick to punish those who failed to celebrate the birth of the Christ Child properly. The seventeenth-century poet Robert Herrick warned that all Christmas greenery should be removed by Twelfth Night or:

> For look! How many leaves there be
> Neglected there, Maids, trust to me,
> So many goblins shall you see.

In Greece, however, half-human, half-animal Christmas goblins called *Kallikantzaroi* wreak havoc at night *during* the Twelve Days of Christmas by eating all the food and breaking furniture. It is only after the blessing of the waters on the Feast of the Epiphany that they are driven back to the center of the earth. The same thing is supposed to happen to the Russian *Leshy*, goat-footed woodland sprites.[7]

In Iceland, the Yule Lads (*Jólasveinar*) were originally goblins born of the child-eating ogres Gryla and Leppaludi. Tales about "these ogres were so blood-chilling that the Danish government, which ruled Iceland in the eighteenth century, legislated in 1746 against using them to frighten children."[8] Fortunately, the nineteenth century reformed the Yule Lads and turned them into impish but benevolent gift-givers (see Chapter Six).

MUTANT ST. LUCYS

St. Lucy of Syracruse is almost literally a beacon of light. As we have seen, her name means light in Latin and her feast day of December 13 used to fall on the winter solstice before the Gregorian reform of the calendar moved the shortest day of the year to December 21. But because of Lucy's association with the solstice, which was considered a hotbed of demonic activity, she sometimes got confused with the bad guys. In some parts of Germany, Lutzelfrau is a flying witch who must be bribed with gifts; in Iceland, Lucy is an ogre; and in some parts of Central Europe, she is—of all things—a nanny goat who rewards good children and threatens to disembowel the bad.[9]

MUTANT ST. MARTIN

St. Lucy is not alone. In Chapter Five we described how St. Nicholas was transformed into Pelznickel and other furry and ferocious sidekicks for himself; here we note that the same thing happened to St. Martin of Tours, who plays a minor role of being the miraculous gift-giver on the eve of his November 11 feast day. In those areas where St. Martin gives gifts, a mysterious figure named Pelzmartin or Pelzmärtel sometimes accompanies or even replaces him. Pelzmartin ("furry Martin" or "spanking Martin") is clad in animal hides and carries a sack and a rod. The rod is for punishing naughty children, and the sack can serve double duty—to carry gifts, or as a means of abducting brats. In some places, parents invite Pelzmartin to the house to criticize and praise the children for their behavior and to distribute presents. How did a saint as generous as Martin of Tours become the victim of such distortion? It seems that even during Christmastime, no good deed goes unpunished.

MUTANT ST. NICHOLASES

See Chapter Five.

WEREWOLVES

Who knew that Christmas was such a dangerous time? Even the werewolves are on the prowl in Yuletide—or at least they were in the Middle Ages in places like Prussia,

Lithuania, Latvia, and Estonia. According to one legend, werewolves gathered on Christmas night and attacked isolated homesteads with great ferocity, hoping to break in and eat all the inhabitants. According to another, a strange boy with a limp wandered the countryside at Christmas summoning the Devil's many followers. Those who lagged behind were scourged with an iron whip. After all were assembled, they turned into wolves and stayed that way for twelve days. Still another legend claims that werewolves gathered for games at a certain castle during Christmastime. "Those too fat to leap over a wall were eaten by their fitter comrades."[10]

WITCHES

In the pre-Christian era, Samhain (better known to you and me as Halloween) may have marked the beginning of the season when witches were most active, but it did not mark the end. The longer the night, the more opportunity for a witch, but when the nights grow shorter after the winter solstice, it only makes witches more irritable. Specific witches such as Lutzelfrau and Berchta terrorized different parts of Europe (see above), but most witches were unnamed. Different "saining" customs were devised to ward off these infestations, including incensing or fumigating, "burning the bush," and making loud noises (see "Devils" above). In Norway, it was considered wise to keep brooms put away lest witches find them and start flying around the house and knocking down the china.

A fire should also be kept burning all night to prevent them from coming down the chimney, and it was a good idea to add salt or dry spruce to the fire to produce an abundance of sparks. During the "Rough Nights" in Austria, locals fought fire with fire. Masquerading as devils and witches, they walked down the streets with brooms, "literally sweeping away unwanted spirits."[11] And have you heard about the New Year's Day superstition "first-footing"? It is supposed to be bad luck if a woman is the first person to enter a house in the new year (see Chapter Twelve for more details). In Wales, the antidote was to have a group of little boys go through the house in a process called "breaking the witch."

Chapter Eight

DECKING THE HALLS: CHRISTMAS TREES, CHRISTMAS PLANTS, AND THE ANSWER TO THE QUESTION IN THE TITLE OF THIS BOOK

The glory of Lebanon shall come to thee, the fir tree, and the box tree, and the pine tree together, to beautify the place of my sanctuary.

—ISAIAH 60:13

In the northern countries, Christmas is a season of more festivity than in those tropical lands where palms bask in the sun, and gorgeous flowers are the story of the whole year. Coming just as Winter has commenced his icy reign, the inner warmth, and glow, and comfort make a deeper impression on the soul, moving it to thankfulness and rejoicing; and branches and wreaths of evergreen form a more fitting decoration in honor of our Saviour's birth, than all the wealth of tropical flowers, which blossom only to wither and perish in an hour.

—*"CHRISTMAS,"* The Aldine, *December 1871*[1]

I t is a natural human impulse to ward off the doldrums of winter by decorating one's home with plants, and evergreens are a natural choice since they are the only plants showing any signs of life at this time of year. These decorations often had no religious meaning but were simply meant to bring cheer in the midst of cold and dark. But sometimes they did: laurel, for instance, was used as a decoration during the Roman Saturnalia, and mistletoe was held sacred by the Druids. As a result, early Christians were wary of using them—at least until they could be properly "baptized." But baptized they were: the old symbolism was modified and given new purpose in light of the Light of the world. The use of other Christmas plants—including the most famous one of all—is a purely Christian invention.

CANDLEMAS BELLS

The feast that falls on February 2 is known by many titles: the Purification of the Blessed Virgin Mary, the Presentation of Our Lord in the Temple, and the

Encounter of Our Lord with Simeon the Prophet. One popular name for the feast is the Mass of Candles, or "Candlemas," because of the elaborate candlelight processions and the blessing of candles that take place on that day. The feast also has its own flower, the snowdrop or Candlemas bells (*Galanthus nivalis*). The pure white flower was seen as a symbol of Mary's purity and was a reminder that although Mary dutifully went to the Temple to obey the Mosaic laws of postpartum purification, she who was conceived without original sin (according to Catholic belief) was in no need of it.

CHRISTMAS PLANTS

It is not surprising that at least a dozen plants have been named after a holiday as popular as Christmas. Most of them, such as the Christmas cactus (*Schlumbergera, varii*), Christmas daisy (*Aster grandiflorus*), Christmas fern (*Polystichum acrostichoides*), and Christmas bush (*Ceratopetalum gummiferum*), take their names from the time of the year when they bloom or from the fact that they are still green during the Christmas season.

CHRISTMAS ROSE

Helleborus niger is variously known as the Christmas flower, Christmas herb, Holy Night rose, rose de Noël or, most commonly, the Christmas rose. It most likely takes these names from the fact that it blooms at

Christmastime, but there is also a rich repertoire of legends attached to it. Several medieval mystery plays, for example, tell the story of Madelon, a young shepherd girl who tagged behind the other shepherds to whom the angel had appeared as they made their way to the manger. Madelon watched as the shepherds played lullabies on their rustic pipes and as the three kings gave gifts of gold, frankincense, and myrrh. Because she had nothing to offer, she was filled with sorrow and began to weep. Suddenly the angel Gabriel appeared to her and asked her why she was crying. "Because," she replied, "I have nothing to offer the Infant Jesus. If only I had some flowers to give him I should be happy, but it is winter, and the frost is on the ground." Gabriel then took Madelon's hand and led her away to a secluded spot. The cold seemed to vanish as they were enveloped in a bright, warm light. Gabriel touched the frozen earth with his staff, and suddenly there appeared white blossoms tinged with pink. Madelon gratefully gathered the roses in her arms and took them to the manger, where she decorated Jesus' crib.[2]

CHRISTMAS TREE

Theories abound about the origins of the world's most famous Christmas plant. The most popular explanation is that the Christmas tree is an extension of the Germanic yuletide tradition of bringing evergreens into the home. But the Yule tree had no religious meaning; it was more like a temporary house plant. And the Yule tree was never decorated, as covering it in decorations would have ruined the point of seeing its life and greenness in the midst of winter's death. In fact, in some parts of Germany Yule trees and Christmas trees literally stood side by side—suggesting two different origins and two different purposes.

There are also claims that specific (Christian) figures—St. Boniface, St. Ansgar, Martin Luther, or even the Christ Child Himself—are responsible for the Christmas tree. But there is little evidence for these assertions.

The most plausible theory is that the Christmas tree is a fusion of two different traditions, both of them Christian: the Paradise Tree and the Christmas Pyramid.

In the Byzantine rite of the Christian East, the Feast of Adam and Eve falls on December 24. A *feast*, you say? Are they not mankind's first sinners? They are, but according to an old tradition they felt really, really bad about the Fall and lived their remaining nine hundred years or so in penance. The Eastern churches placed their feast on December 24 as a reminder of why Christ was born: "God and sinner reconciled," as the famous carol puts it.

The Feast of Adam and Eve has never been on the Western Church calendar, but in the Middle Ages, mystery plays were staged on Christmas Eve day that included a Paradise tree, a tree representing both the Tree of the Knowledge of Good and Evil as well as the Tree of Life from the Garden of Eden (Genesis 2:9). The tree was fir, and it was decorated with red apples to symbolize the forbidden fruit that Eve ate (from the Tree of the Knowledge of Good and Evil) and with unconsecrated wafers to symbolize the Holy Eucharist (so that the tree also stood for the Tree of Life). The wafers were eventually replaced with candy to represent the sweetness of Christ's redemption. The idea of edible decorations, by the way, endured into the twentieth century. (The reason Animal Crackers have a string on their box is that they were invented as a seasonal treat to be hung on the Christmas tree.)

By the fifteenth century, because abuses had crept into the Adam and Eve mystery plays, the Church suppressed their performance. Folks in western Germany, however, were so fond of the Paradise tree that they moved it from the stage to their homes.

The second tradition is of a Christmas light as a symbol of Christ. Some Christians lit a Christmas candle on Christmas Eve and prayed around it through the night. In western Germany, the Christmas light took the form of a "Christmas Pyramid" (*Weihnachtspyramide*), a wooden triangular structure bedecked with small candles, evergreen twigs, glass balls, and tinsel, with the Star of Bethlehem on top. The pyramid symbolized the coming of the Light of the World, but the various candles also represented Jesus Christ's ancestors, his "Jesse Tree" (see Chapter Two). There was often a Nativity set underneath the Christmas pyramid.

Beginning in the sixteenth century, the inhabitants of western Germany, on the left bank of the Rhine, began to combine these December 24 traditions, taking the Paradise Tree and adorning it with lights, a star, and tinsel. The apples were replaced with glass balls and the sweets with candy canes. Lights were transferred to the tree and the star placed on top of it. The nativity set went from under the pyramid to under the tree. By the seventeenth century, the Christmas tree was com-

"Bringing Home a Christmas Tree" by Mary Mapes Dodge. *St. Nicholas: An Illustrated Magazine for Young Folks*

plete—more or less. As late as the nineteenth century some Americans and Germans had figures of Adam and Eve and the serpent under the tree, a lingering holdover from the Paradise Tree.

The new custom caught on gradually. It was not until the nineteenth century that all of Germany and some Slavic lands had embraced it. Princess Helen of Mecklenburg brought it to France in 1837, and Queen Victoria's husband, the German-born Prince Albert, introduced it to England in 1841 when he had a tree set up at Windsor Castle. North America first saw the Christmas tree in the 1700s when Protestant Germans from the Rhine settled in western Pennsylvania—or, some say, when Hessian mercenaries fighting for the British set up the first Christmas tree near Trenton, New Jersey, in December 1776. But it was really the second wave of German immigrants in the 1830s that popularized the custom in the U.S., from centers like Holy Trinity German Catholic Church in Boston. And when the custom stuck, it stuck: in 1850 Charles Dickens called the Christmas tree "a new German toy," but by 1891 President Benjamin Harrison was calling it "old-fashioned."[3]

As we saw in Chapter One, in 1912 Boston became the first city in the world to have public Christmas trees. The two most famous in the United States today are probably the National Christmas Tree in Washington, D.C., and the Rockefeller Center Christmas Tree in midtown Manhattan. The National Christmas Tree, currently located in the northeast quadrant of the Ellipse near the White House, is an evergreen tree lit by the president of the United States during a public ceremony. The annual tradition began in 1923 and has mostly involved living rather than cut trees. For the first three decades the tree was lit on the traditional date of December 24; since then, the date of the ceremony has varied. The Rockefeller Center Christmas Tree tradition began in 1933 when a fifty-foot Balsam fir was put up in Rockefeller Center. Today the donated tree is erected in mid-November and first lit the Wednesday after Thanksgiving in a public ceremony that is broadcast by NBC. The tree can be no taller than one hundred feet because Manhattan's streets are so narrow that they will not allow for anything taller to be transported. After the tree is taken down on New Year's Day, it is turned into lumber that is donated to Habitat for Humanity.

In 1982, Polish-born Pope St. John Paul II introduced the northern European custom to the Vatican when he had a Christmas tree and nativity scene set up in St. Peter's Square. Now an annual tradition, it has become an honor for a different country each year to donate the tree to the pope. In 2020, Slovenia donated a spruce tree that was ninety feet high, seventy-five years old, and weighed seven tons.

Public Christmas trees can also be tokens of gratitude. Olso, Norway, gives a Christmas tree every year to London's Trafalgar Square in thanksgiving for British support of the Norwegian resistance during World War II, and Bergen, Norway, gives a tree to Newcastle, England, because of the role Newcastle soldiers played in liberating their city. Norway also gives Washington, D.C., an annual Christmas tree as a token of friendship and in gratitude for U.S. aid in liberating Norway from Nazi occupation. The province of Nova Scotia, Canada, donates a tree to Boston in remembrance of that city's rapid assistance after an ammunition ship explosion leveled the city of Halifax in 1917.

From its beginnings in the sixteenth century until the 1960s or so, the Christmas tree was not decorated or lit until the evening of December 24: trimming the tree was once a cherished Christmas Eve tradition that took on almost a ritual aspect. The tree would be kept up throughout the Twelve Days of Christmas and serve not only as the location for presents but as a centerpiece for family prayer.

CHRISTMAS WREATH

The Christmas wreath, a garland usually made with holly and other evergreens, may have been introduced to the U.S. by immigrants from Ireland and England, but its origins are obscure. Some suggest that it is a joyful variation of the funeral wreath that used to hang on the door of a household suffering the loss of a loved one. What is certain is that the wreath is a symbol of victory (see "Laurel" below) and, because of its circular shape, of eternity. In Christian art, wreaths have been linked to the martyrs, who were victorious over their tormentors in not betraying Christ. The Christmas wreath recalls the birth of the eternally begotten Son of God as well as the crown of thorns He would come to wear.

CHRYSANTHEMUM

Chrysanthemums are not often used as Christmas decorations, but perhaps they should be. According to legend, this star-shaped flower was useful to the Wise Men. When the Magi reached Bethlehem, they got lost in the dark until Melchior discovered a chrysanthemum and picked it. Immediately the doors of a nearby stable flew open, revealing the Holy Family.

HOLLY

The common European holly (*Ilex aquifolium*) and American or Christmas holly (*Ilex opaca*) became Christmas garlands not as a holdover from pagan yuletide customs but because of their symbolic value. With the rest of the forest brown or blanketed with snow, holly is one of the few standouts. In the words of the traditional British carol "The Holly and the Ivy,"

> The holly and the ivy,
> When they are both full grown,
> Of all the trees that are in the wood,
> The holly bears the crown.

Holly's peculiar properties made it a natural for Christmas. Holly's prickly edges and red berries, it is said, point to three things: the thorny bush glowing red with fire that Moses saw on Mt. Horeb, the fiery love for God that filled Mary's heart, and the bloody crown of thorns that the newborn King would one day wear (in fact, in some languages holly is known as "Christ's thorn"). And, in the words of the carol,

> The holly bears a berry
> As red as any blood

And Mary bore sweet Jesus Christ
To do poor sinners good.

The use of holly as an emblem of the Burning Bush is appropriate since some Christians believe that it was not the Trinity or God the Father Who appeared to Moses in the Burning Bush, but God the Son—the same God Who would become a helpless babe in a manger. The Burning Bush is also seen as a type of the Blessed Virgin Mary, whose virginity was preserved despite childbirth just as the bush was preserved despite the fire's engulfing it.

"The Holly and the Ivy" offers additional symbolic interpretations:

The holly bears a blossom,
As white as the lily flower,
And Mary bore sweet Jesus Christ,
To be our sweet Saviour. . . .

The holly bears a prickle,
As sharp as any thorn,
And Mary bore sweet Jesus Christ
On Christmas Day in the morn. . . .

The holly bears a bark,
As bitter as any gall,

And Mary bore sweet Jesus Christ
For to redeem us all. . . .

Besides its symbolic potential, holly also has
superstition on its side. In Germany, holly used
as a decoration in church was brought home as a
charm against lightning and the evil eye. In medieval
England, attaching a sprig of holly to the bed at
Christmas protected a young maiden all year round
from being turned into a witch by the Evil One. The
English also believed that good luck was brought to
men by holly and to women by ivy. Hence these lines
from "The Contest of the Ivy and the Holly":

Holly and his merry men they dance and
    sing,
Ivy and her maidens weep, and hands
    wring.

Whatever the reasons, next to the Christmas tree
holly is the symbol par excellence of Christmas joy:
when the hall is decked with boughs of holly, you know
that now it is the season to be jolly. We suspect that
holly's popularity is the reason that red and green are
the unofficial colors of Christmas (that, and perhaps the
Paradise Tree), even though the liturgical color for the
season is white.

IVY

Ivy (*Hedera helix*) was originally banned from Christian homes because of its associations with Roman bacchanalia, festivities honoring the wine god Bacchus; because of this association, ivy had become a symbol of unrestrained eating and drinking (superstitiously, wearing it was supposed to prevent drunkenness). It took several centuries for the distaste of this symbolism to wear off. Even during the Middle Ages ivy hardly ever appeared as a Christmas decoration on the Continent, while in England it was restricted to outdoor use. As "The Contest of the Ivy and the Holly" says,

> Holly stands in the hall, fair to behold;
> Ivy stands without the door, she is full sore
>   a-cold.

Another mark against ivy was the fact that it was often found in English cemeteries and hence had come to be associated with death. As Charles Dickens wrote in "The Ivy Green,"

> Creeping where no life is seen,
> A rare old plant is the ivy green.

Eventually, however, ivy's qualities were appreciated anew. Seeing its tenacious clinging to rock as a symbol of fidelity and an allegory for human dependence on divine strength, Christians made ivy a popular Christmas symbol as well as a favorite indoor plant year round. And once it became popular, new popular customs grew up around it. In Oxfordshire in the seventeenth century, if a woman asked a man for Christmas ivy and he did not provide it, she had the right to nail his britches to the gate and deny him "the well-known privilege of the mistletoe."[4]

LAUREL

Laurel or bay (*Laurus nobilis*) also initially suffered from its ties to the old pagan religion. Because it was a favorite decoration used during the Roman Saturnalia (celebrated December 17–23), the early Church frowned upon its use. "Let those who face the fire of hell affix laurels to their doorposts," harrumphed Tertullian (155–240). "You are a light of the world, a tree ever green; if you have renounced the pagan temple, make not your home such a temple!"[5]

But ironically, the evergreen bay was a concrete symbol that Christians could use to express the very point Tertullian was making. Laurel also betokened purity, prosperity, and health, and it was the ancient Roman symbol of victory: winners of athletic contests in ancient Greece were crowned with laurel wreaths, and Roman Emperors used laurel trees to reinforce their status as winners favored by Apollo. These associations still linger in our language. One theory about the word "baccalaureate" is that it comes from *bacca lauri* or "laurel berry" for a student successfully attaining his or her first degree (Italian university students who just graduated still wear laurel wreaths), while a "poet laureate" is literally a poet crowned with laurels.[6] And "to rest on one's laurels" means to rely on one's past achievements.

As the old saying has it, to the victor go the spoils, and after Christianity triumphed over its pagan adversary in the Roman Empire, it took this symbol of victory and imperial might and gave it to the newborn King lying in the manger. Laurel thus became the first plant to be used as a Christmas decoration.

MISTLETOE

It's funny how such a nice Christmas tradition involves such a naughty plant. European mistletoe (*Viscum album*) and its North American counterparts (members of the genus *Phoradendron*) are parasites. The mistletoe plant drills *haustoria* or sinkers into the living tissue of a branch in order to extract water and nutrients. The more mistletoe on a tree, the less chance a tree has of surviving (the genus *Phoradendron* is Greek for "tree thief"). Mistletoe does, however, have pretty little flowers in the late fall or winter that are soon followed by white berries. Birds eat those berries and then rub their seed-laden beaks or deposit their seed-rich droppings on other branches. This twofold way of dissemination may account for its name in English. The "mistle" in mistletoe could be in reference to the mistle thrush (*Turdus viscivorus* or "mistletoe-eating thrush"), which, as its name implies, loves to snack on the parasite; or, "mistel-toe" could be (highly descriptive) Anglo-Saxon for "dung on a twig."

The Druids were a little more romantic with their nomenclature. Their name for mistletoe, which they bequeathed to the Irish Gaelic language, means "All-Healer"—or, if you will, "Cure All." Those "white-robed men of the sickle and the mistletoe," as the novelist Evelyn Waugh called them,[7] were fascinated by this weird and seemingly miraculous plant that grows without soil, staying green and even bearing fruit in the dead of winter. The druids would climb oak trees to harvest mistletoe in the moonlight with a golden sickle, careful never to let it touch the ground. Then they sacrificed two white bulls and held a feast. The mistletoe would later be used in a drink to cure infertility and counteract poison.[8] (Although mistletoe is considered mildly toxic, the Druids may have been onto something: mistletoe can lower blood pressure and the heart rate, and some researchers think it can cure cancer or at least counteract the ill effects of chemotherapy.) The Druids are said to have harvested mistletoe around New Year's Day, which may explain the custom in some areas of not hanging mistletoe until New Year's Eve. "Hogmanay," the Scottish word for New Year's Eve, may in fact be derived from the old French, *Au gui l'an neuf*, "To the mistletoe! The new year!"[9]

The Romans liked mistletoe, too; according to the legend of the Golden Bough it was a portal to the underworld. But they were also practical. They made birdlime (a sticky substance that works like flypaper) out of the mucilage of mistletoe berries to trap the very birds that spread the plant through their dung. The irony was not lost: a Latin expression for being hoisted with one's own petard is *Turdus ipse sibi malum cacat*: "It is the thrush itself that poops its own doom."

But how, you ask, did mistletoe go from pecking into bark to people pecking under it? The origin of the popular Christmas custom is not a settled question, we have to admit. We do know intriguing details of the development of the tradition, though. For example, the significance of kissing under the mistletoe has changed over time. As one scholar explains, originally "a kiss under the mistletoe was interpreted as a sincere pledge of love and a promise of marriage, and, at the same time, it was an omen of happiness, good fortune, fertility, and long life to the lovers who sealed and made known their engagement by a kiss beneath" it.[10] But why mistletoe, in the first place? The Druids never kissed under the mistletoe, but they did associate the plant—which, as we have seen, is evergreen, grows without soil, and bears blooms and berries in the dead of winter—with fertility. And there was also an ancient custom whereby two enemies who happened to meet under the "sacred mistletoe" laid down their arms, exchanged a friendly greeting, and kept a truce for the rest of the day. Finally, there is a Scandinavian myth about the god Loki tricking the god Hoder into killing the god Baldr or Balder with a mistletoe arrow. Then when Baldr was brought back to life, the mistletoe—contrite for its role in his death—promised that it would never do harm again as long as it did not touch the ground.[11] The mistletoe thus went from being an agent of death to a symbol of resurrection, life, and love.

Our own guess is that Christians, drawing from these associations, added the kiss. If mistletoe could occasion a truce, it would not be difficult to upgrade the meaning to the peace that the world cannot give (John 14:27) with a quintessentially Christian "kiss of peace," a tradition that goes back to the New Testament (see Romans 16:16). And if mistletoe betokened fertility, then let that fertility happen within the holy sacrament of matrimony. It is appropriate that the holy kiss would find its way under the leafy broker of peace during the season celebrating how God kissed the world through the birth of His Son in order to give it peace—even if that holy kiss has gotten a little unholy at times, through too much eggnog-induced enthusiasm.

And Christians added some lore of their own. According to one tale, because mistletoe was once the mightiest tree on earth, its hard and heavy wood was used to make Christ's cross. When Jesus died and the sky was dark and the earth shook and the graves gave up their dead, all the mistletoe trees around the world shriveled up and died from shame. But Jesus took pity on the mistletoe. Assuring it that it was not to blame, He gathered its shriveled remains and placed it on the branches of other trees for support. And the Lord gave the mistletoe an additional blessing to show that He held no grudges: He would have mistletoe at His birthday celebrations as a reminder for folks to love each other and be gentle to each other like the Baby Jesus.[12] As a result of legends like this, mistletoe in some places was called *herbe de la croix* (herb of the cross) and *lignum crucis* (wood of the cross) and described as a symbol of the Tree of Life:

> The mistletoe bough at our Christmas board
> Shall hang, to the honor of Christ the Lord:
> For He is the evergreen tree of Life.[13]

Mistletoe is hung in the doorway of a home or in the middle of a room; the suspension from above harks to its natural place in the trees, and it keeps the mistletoe from touching the ground and causing bad luck. Interestingly churches, which have no problem with holly and other evergreens, have tended to shy away from the plant because it had been a principal pagan symbol—either that, or they don't want smooching going on in the pews. There are, however, exceptions to this rule. Beginning in the Middle Ages in the

Cathedral of York, a large bundle of mistletoe was solemnly placed on the altar by a priest and treated as a symbol of Christ. The tradition continues to this day, along with a proclamation for "public and universal liberty, pardon and freedom of all sorts of inferior and wicked people at the Minster steps, and the gates of the City, towards the four quarters of Heaven"—that is, amnesty for local criminals who came to the Minster. The Druidic "Cure-All" has found its fulfillment in the forgiving newborn King Whom one Advent hymn calls the "Cure for a sick world" (*languidi mundi Medela*).

Christmas Eve was traditionally the earliest time to hang up mistletoe, along with other evergreens. Some English shires insisted that mistletoe should only go up on New Year's Eve, and one outlier region did not put up its mistletoe until Twelfth Night (January 5). Most Englishmen and their American cousins would take their mistletoe down on Epiphany (January 6) or Candlemas Eve (February 1) or Candlemas Day (February 2), but a few kept theirs up the entire year as protection, replacing it each Christmastime. Try this today, however, and you won't be seen as a peacemaker but a lazy bum, like the neighbor who never takes the Christmas lights down from his roof gutters.

It is mildly amusing to observe how the rules for kissing under the mistletoe have been relaxed over the years. As previously mentioned, it is speculated that the first mistletoe kisses were essentially marriage proposals. By the early nineteenth century in England and America, men were allowed to kiss multiple maidens under the mistletoe, but each time they did they had to pluck one of the berries from the bunch; when all the berries were gone, so too were the kissing rights. Although this restraint is no longer observed, focus on the mistletoe today tends to be on friendly kisses as a token of peace and good will to all guests entering the home. But of course there will always be show-offs. During their annual Brewery Lights holiday celebration on December 7, 2019, Anheuser-Busch set the record for the most couples kissing in the same place under the mistletoe (480) and the most couples kissing under the mistletoe in multiple venues (896).[14] The single-venue record was set at their location in St. Louis, Missouri, and the multiple-venue record was set with the help of their breweries in Merrimack, New Hampshire, and Fort Collins, Colorado. In Merrimack, the event retrieved mistletoe's older meaning in at least one case: it led to a marriage proposal. The previous multiple-venue record had been held by seven Six Flags amusement parks in 2016 when 839 couples held hands and kissed for at least ten seconds under a live mistletoe. That event, too, inspired a man to drop a knee and pop the question.[15]

POINSETTIA

A more recent addition to the Christmas plant pageant is the glorious poinsettia (*Euphorbia pulcherrima*) from Mexico and Central America. The plant's name in English pays tribute to Joel Roberts Poinsett, the United States' first Minister to Mexico, who is credited with introducing it to the United States in the 1820s (December 12, the anniversary of Poinsett's death, is National Poinsettia Day). In Mexico, Guatemala, and Ecuador, however, the plant is *la flor de Nochebuena* or the flower of Holy Night. No matter that the plant's flaming red "petals" are actually its leaves: the poinsettia is an apt reminder of the star that led the Wise Men to Bethlehem, while its red color (according to the traditional explanation) betokens the Precious Blood that Jesus Christ would shed for the redemption of many.

The Aztecs were the first to cultivate poinsettias for red dye and to reduce fevers, but according to a sixteenth-century legend, the plant is the product of a Christmas miracle. One day a little girl named Maria or Pepita was crying because she was too poor to give Jesus a gift on his birthday. An angel instructed her to gather weeds and place them in front of the church altar. The child obeyed, and the weeds turned into a poinsettia. We do know that Franciscan friars in Mexico were using the plants as Christmas decorations as early as the seventeenth century. Today approximately seventy million poinsettias are sold in the United States every year in the six weeks around Christmas.

RADISHES?

December 23 in Oaxaca, Mexico, is the Night of the Radishes (*Noche de Rábanos*), a festival and a competition to see who has the best carved large radish (*Raphanus sativus*). The annual event can be traced back to the colonial era, when the Spaniards' introduction of radishes to the region met the locals' skills in woodcarving. Farmers would carve radishes to attract attention to their stands at the Christmas market held on December 23, and eventually they began to compete against each other. The competition was made formal by the city in 1897. Radishes do not keep well—they wilt quickly once they are cut—so the competition can only last for a few hours. Every year thousands of visitors wait in lines for as long as five hours to see all the contest entries.

ROSEMARY

As a Christmas symbol, rosemary (*Rosemarinus officianalis*) is almost as old as laurel. Medieval legend ascribes protection against evil spirits to rosemary that is used as a decoration in church on Christmas Day. In the seventeenth century, it was considered one of the essentials of Christmas décor:

With holly and ivy
So green and so gay,
We deck up our houses
As fresh as the day;
With bays and rosemary,
And laurel compleate,
And every one now
Is a king in conceite.[16]

An ancient legend explaining the reason for its use at Christmastime claims that when the Holy Family was fleeing to Egypt, Mary stopped along the way, washed Jesus' tiny clothes, and spread them out to dry on a rosemary bush. God rewarded the bush with a pleasing fragrance. Similarly, when the Blessed Mother threw her purple cloak on the bush during the same flight into Egypt, God changed the color of its flowers from white to lavender. *Rosemarinus* means "dew of the sea" in Latin, but English-speakers think of it as "Mary's rose."

Inexplicably, rosemary fell into decline as a Christmas decoration in the nineteenth century; today its use at Christmas is largely confined to cooking.

Chapter Nine

NOT-SO-SILENT NIGHT: FAMOUS CHRISTMAS CAROLS

W hether it is secular songs on the radio, religious hymns in church, or carolers on the street, no other time of year is so marked by special music as Christmas. Of course, these are two different cycles: radio stations begin inundating the air waves with Christmas songs by the likes of Gene Autry, Bing Crosby, the Pogues, and Mariah Carey the day after Thanksgiving, and they end promptly at the end of Christmas Day. Christian congregations and carolers, on the other hand, traditionally begin singing their Christmas songs on

Christmas Day and typically continue until Epiphany on January 6.

The Christmas musical collection is vast: in this chapter we will limit ourselves to the English-language Christmas carols most popular in America today. And since the word "carol" has undergone quite a transformation over the centuries, we lazily refrain from making a distinction between a hymn, a song, and a carol. Derived from the Greek words for "dance" (*choros*) and "play the flute" (*aulein*), a carol was originally a dance, usually performed in a circle, to the accompaniment of flute music. Medieval England dropped the flute requirement and made a carol a ring dance accompanied by singing. By this definition, only something like the nursery game "Ring-a-Round the Rosie" would qualify as a true carol. Over time, however, "carol" came to refer to a song—typically a song more festive or playful and less solemn than a hymn, but the line between the two can be thin. A carol—"Jingle Bells," to give one example—need not have religious content. Caroling does, however, retain a vestige of its kinetic dance roots, at least insofar as Christmas caroling implies sauntering from house to house.

Christmas carols have had a tumultuous history. Beautiful Christmas hymns that celebrate the theological meaning of the Lord's Incarnation and Nativity were being written as early as the fifth century. St. Francis of Assisi (d. 1226), however, shifted the focus to the sights and sounds of the first Christmas: to the stable, the hay, the poor couple, and a helpless baby shivering in the cold. This attention to concrete details of the birth, combined with a sense of joy and affection, became *the* template for Christmas carols. It caught on throughout Catholic Europe and then Lutheran Germany, but it ran afoul of later Protestants: the early Calvinists preferred metrical psalms, and Puritans preferred no Christmas music whatsoever. The Methodists of the eighteenth century, however, revived caroling in England, and the nineteenth-century Episcopalians and Anglicans added to our repertoire of fine Christmas music. As a result, today's Christmas songbook reflects a wide array of contributors: Catholic saints and Protestant Reformers, famous poets and lowly copyeditors, distinguished music professionals and rank amateurs, English noblemen and African slaves. Clergy and laity, highborn and lowborn, male and female, black and white, Christian and, as we will see, Jew—it is as if Christmas music fulfills the Biblical prophecies of a great multitude from every background singing out to God and His Son.

ANGELS WE HAVE HEARD ON HIGH

Les Anges dans nos campagnes is a traditional sixteenth-century French or Flemish "antiphon hymn," a hymn inspired by one of the antiphon verses used in sacred liturgy (in this case, from the Office of Lauds on Christmas Day). In 1862 James Chadwick, the Catholic Bishop of Hexham and Newcastle in northeast England, loosely translated the lyrics into English, and in 1937 the American composer Edward Shippen Barnes arranged the beautiful chorus of *Gloria in excelsis Deo*, which sustains a melodic cascade of sixteen notes on the "o." The first verse is:

> Angels we have heard on high
> Sweetly singing o'er the plains
> And the mountains in reply
> Echoing their joyous strains
> *Gloria in excelsis Deo!*
> *Gloria in excelsis Deo!*

AWAY IN A MANGER

This hymn used to be called "Luther's Cradle Song" because it was erroneously believed to have been composed by Martin Luther for his children. (That said, Luther's Christmas hymn *Vom Himmel kam der Engel Schar,* which includes the verse "Away there in the manger a little Infant lies" may have helped inspire it.) Nineteenth-century German Lutherans in Pennsylvania are the most likely authors of this popular hymn, which first appeared in print in 1882 and has several textual variations. It also has at least forty-one musical settings, the two most popular being by James R. Murray in 1887 and William James Kirkpatrick in 1895. The first verse (from Kirkpatrick's version) is:

> Away in a manger, no crib for a bed,

The little Lord Jesus laid down His sweet
   head.
The stars in the bright sky
looked down where He lay,
The little Lord Jesus asleep on the hay.

CAROL OF THE BELLS

In 1914, Ukrainian composer Mykola Leontovych arranged a Ukrainian folk chant called *Shchedryk* ("Bountiful Evening"), which tells the story of a little swallow flying into a home and singing about wealth in the coming spring. The song was originally sung on the evening of January 13, which ushers in the new year according to the Julian calendar.

In 1921, Peter J. Wilhousky heard Leontovych's arrangement performed by the Ukrainian National Chorus at Carnegie Hall and was impressed. In 1936, he copyrighted his own original lyrics—"Hark how the bells, sweet silver bells...."—under the title "Carol of the Bells." Wilhousky, the arranger for the NBC Symphony Orchestra, centered the song on bells because the urgent, jumpy melody reminded him of hand bells.

The carol has proved quite versatile: it has been performed as classical music, heavy metal, rock, pop, jazz, and country and has made numerous appearances in film and TV. John Williams made a fetching arrangement of the carol for the 1990 Christmas classic *Home Alone*, and a hard rock version by Trans-Siberian Orchestra inspired an air-guitar jam session led by Dwight Schrute in the 2011 "Christmas Wishes" episode of *The Office*.

CAROL OF THE DRUM

See "The Little Drummer Boy" below.

THE CHRISTMAS SONG

Also known as "Chestnuts Roasting on an Open Fire" and "Merry Christmas to You," the carol officially known as "The Christmas Song" was composed as an attempt to beat the heat. During a brutal July heat wave in California in 1945, Mel Tormé went to visit the home of his writing partner Robert Wells. Wells was nowhere to be found, but on his piano was a spiral pad with four lines scribbled on it: "Chestnuts roasting on an open fire," "Jack Frost nipping at your nose," "Yuletide carols being sung by a choir," and "Folks dressed up as Eskimos." When Wells appeared, he explained to his friend: "You know, Mel, I have tried everything to cool down. I've been in my pool. I had a cold drink. I've taken a cold shower. I'm nothing but hot. And I thought that maybe, you know, if I could just write down a few lines of wintery verse I could psychologically get an edge over this heat."[1]

It's a good thing that Wells did not have air conditioning, or the reputedly most popular Christmas song in the world would not have been written. Tormé immediately saw the musical potential of Wells's psychological exercise, and within forty-five minutes he had written the music and most of the lyrics. The duo wasted no time; later that afternoon they presented it to their friend Nat King Cole. When he heard it, Cole exclaimed, "Stop everything. That's my song!" And boy was he right. Nat King Cole recorded "The Christmas Song" three times—in 1946, 1953, and 1961. The 1961 version, with a full orchestra, arranged and conducted by Ralph Carmichael, is the one you are most likely to hear today.

COME, THOU LONG EXPECTED JESUS

Christmas, as we will explore in detail in Chapter Eleven, celebrates the first coming of Jesus Christ in order to better prepare for His Second Coming. "Come, Thou Long Expected Jesus" is one of the few Christmas carols that draws from this connection. In 1744, Charles Wesley, younger brother of John Wesley, the founder of Methodism, was meditating on Haggai 2:1— "And I will shake all nations, and the desire of all nations shall come: and I will fill this house with glory, saith the Lord of hosts." Saddened by the plight of orphans in his area and the class stratification in Great Britain, Charles Wesley was moved to write "Come, Thou Long Expected Jesus." The first verse is

> Come, Thou long expected Jesus,
> Born to set Thy people free;
> From our fears and sins release us,

Let us find our rest in Thee.
Israel's strength and consolation,
Hope of all the earth Thou art;
Dear desire of every nation,
Joy of every longing heart.

The carol did not catch on as quickly as some others because initially it was not set to a particular melody. Today, the Welsh tune "Hyfrydol" by Rowland H. Prichard is probably the most popular pairing, followed by Christian Friedrich Witt's "Stuttgart."

THE COVENTRY CAROL

The Coventry mystery plays were medieval performances held in Coventry, England, which told the entire life of Christ. One of them, the "Pageant of the Shearman and Tailors" (named after the sponsoring guilds), depicts the events of the second chapter of the Gospel according to Matthew, which includes the massacre of the Holy Innocents by the wicked King Herod. One of the songs from the play, the "Coventry Carol," is a lullaby by the mothers of the children who are doomed to die:

Lully, lullah, thou little tiny child,
Bye bye, lully, lullay.
Thou little tiny child,
Bye bye, lully, lullay.

The mystery plays were performed for the Feast of Corpus Christi in the summer, but eventually the "Coventry Carol" went on to become what it is today: hands down, the most depressing Christmas carol of all time. The song got a boost in popularity in 1940 when the BBC Empire Broadcast concluded its Christmas program with the carol's being sung in the ruins of Coventry Cathedral, which had been bombed by the Germans a month earlier. Even the way in which its popularity spread is depressing!

DO YOU HEAR WHAT I HEAR?

This popular song plays fast and loose with the details of the Christmas story: the night wind tells a lamb about a star, the lamb tells a shepherd boy about a song, the shepherd boy tells "the mighty king" about a Child shivering in the cold, and the king declares that the Child will bring us goodness and light.

But the authors can be forgiven: they were responding to the Cuban Missile Crisis in October 1962. When the king in the song says, "Pray for peace, people everywhere!" the composers really meant it. The song was written by Noël Regnery and Gloria Shayne. (How appropriate is it to have a Christmas carol written by two people named Noël and Gloria? Gloria, by the way, grew up in Brookline, Massachusetts, next door to one of the key players in the Cuban Missile Crisis, President John F. Kennedy.) The composing duo, who were married at the time, were worried about the threat of nuclear war when they came up with their carol.

"Do You Hear What I Hear" was first performed by the Harry Simeone Chorale and released after Thanksgiving 1962. It sold more than a quarter of a million copies during the 1962 Christmas season and became an even bigger hit when Bing Crosby released his own version of it the following year.

DING DONG! MERRILY ON HIGH

This cheery and festive carol is the product of two talented clerics more than three centuries apart. Jehan Tabourot was a sixteenth-century Catholic priest in France who was, you could say, interested in earthly and heavenly dance: the earthly dance of human beings and the heavenly dance of the sun, moon, and stars. Tabourot wrote both a book on astronomy and a study of dance called *Orchésographie*, which includes a catchy melody called "Branle de l'Official." Then, over three hundred years later, in 1924, Anglican minister George Ratcliffe Woodward used the tune for his original composition "Ding Dong! Merrily on High." In addition to being a gifted composer, the Cambridge-educated Woodward was a renowned linguist who translated a large number of hymns from Greek, Latin, and German. His love of archaic poetry no doubt influenced his decision to compose a "macaronic" carol— one that mixes different languages, in this case Latin and the vernacular. It also did not hurt that Woodward had an interest in church bell ringing:

> Ding dong! Merrily on high
> In heav'n the bells are ringing:
> Ding dong! verily the sky
> Is riv'n with angel-singing.
>
> Glo----------------------------ria,
> Hosanna in excelsis!
> Glo----------------------------ria,
> Hosanna in excelsis!

THE FIRST NOEL

You would think that this carol is of French provenance because Noël is the French word for Christmas, but it is Cornish in origin and the proper spelling is "Nowell." In either spelling, it means "News." "The First Nowell" is in fact one of many "Noel" Christmas carols in English and French, all focusing on the Good News of Christ's birth using "Noel" or "Nowell" as a refrain. A different traditional English carol proclaims:

> Noel, Noel, Noel,
> Tidings good I think to tell.
> The boar's head that we bring here,
>
> Betokeneth a prince without peer

Is born today to buy us dear.
Noel, Noel, Noel.

Whereas the first verse of the famous "First Nowell" carol is:

The first Nowell the angel did say
Was to certain poor shepherds in fields as
  they lay;
In fields where they lay, keeping their
  sheep,
On a cold winter's night that was so deep:
Nowell, Nowell, Nowell, Nowell,
Born is the King of Israel.

GO, TELL IT ON THE MOUNTAIN

One of the treasures of American music is the Negro spiritual, and the best-known Christmas carol in this tradition is "Go, Tell It on the Mountain." The version with which most of us are familiar was arranged by John W. Work Jr. (1872–1925), who studied classics at Harvard University and taught Latin, Greek, and history at Fisk University in Nashville from 1898–1923. Its refrain is:

Go, tell it on the mountain,
Over the hills and everywhere;
Go, tell it on the mountain
That Jesus Christ is born!

(Substitute "born" for "Lord," and you have a hymn for all year round.)

GOD REST YE MERRY, GENTLEMEN

One of the oldest English Christmas carols still in use, "God Rest Ye Merry, Gentlemen" hails from the sixteenth century or maybe even earlier: it was already being called "the old Christmas carol" in the mid-seventeen-hundreds. The original punctuation of this carol is not "God rest ye, merry gentlemen" but "God rest ye merry, gentlemen," which means "God keep you in peace, gentlemen":

> God rest ye merry, gentlemen
> Let nothing you dismay
> For Jesus Christ our Saviour
> Was born on Christmas Day
> To save us all from Satan's pow'r
> When we were gone astray
> O tidings of comfort and joy
> Comfort and joy
> O tidings of comfort and joy.

The song is in the minority for being in a minor key: most Christmas carols are sung to a major melody. You may have noticed that not all the lyrics rhyme, for example:

> The shepherds at those tidings

Rejoiced much in mind,
And left their flocks a-feeding
In tempest, storm and wind,
And went to Bethlehem straightway
The Son of God to find.

For that you can blame the "Great Vowel Shift," a series of changes that took place in the English language from the fifteenth to the eighteenth century. At the time that the carol was composed, "wind" was pronounced like "mind" and "find."

GOOD KING WENCESLAUS

John Mason Neale was an Anglican priest and a talented English hymn writer. As a member of the Oxford Movement, he was interested in reincorporating Catholic elements into the Church of England. In 1849 he published a book recounting the lives of holy men and women, including St. Wenceslaus I (d. 935), the Duke of Bohemia and patron of the Czech Republic who was martyred by his wicked brother Boleslaw the Bad and whose feast day is September 28. Around 1853 Neale was given a rare copy of a Finnish song book from 1582 that contained a lively springtime carol from the thirteenth century. Set in doubled trochaic meter, it was called "Tempus Adest Floridum" or "Eastertime is Here." Neale loved the tune, and in 1853 wrote his own lyrics based on the life of, you guessed it, good King Wenceslaus.

Neale's carol tells the story of Wenceslaus's going out on St. Stephen's Day (December 26), a day traditionally associated with almsgiving (see Chapter Twelve). In the bitter cold he sees a poor peasant and immediately takes him meat, wine, and firewood. The king's page, however, cannot keep up with him in the snow until Wenceslaus suggests he follow in his footsteps. In the words of the last verse:

> In his master's steps he trod
> Where the snow lay dinted.
> Heat was in the very sod
> Which the Saint had printed.
> Therefore, Christian men, be sure,
> Wealth or rank possessing,
> Ye who now will bless the poor
> Shall yourselves find blessing.

While the story is probably fictitious, it artfully includes what we do know about St. Wenceslaus, such as his great charity for the poor and his custom of carrying firewood to them on his own back at night. But two of the lines in the last stanza are particularly telling. How could heat "be in the very sod / Which the Saint had printed?" According to the Roman Breviary, one of the ways Wenceslaus mortified his flesh was by walking barefoot in the snow until "his bloodstained footprints warmed the ground."[2] The footprints are heated, then, by the blood of the saint, whose sacrifice enables others to follow him. Thus, the hymn depicts a medieval king honoring a Biblical saint with his mastery over the flesh and his love for the poor:

> Good King Wenceslaus looked out,
> On the Feast of Stephen,
> When the snow lay round about,
> Deep and crisp and even;
> Brightly shone the moon that night,
> Though the frost was cruel,
> When a poor man came in sight,
> Gath'ring winter fuel.

HARK! THE HERALD ANGELS SING

In 1739, the prolific Charles Wesley, author of an astonishing 6,500 hymns, published "Hymn for Christmas-Day." Wesley's original lyrics were worked over several times, giving us "Hark! The Herald Angels Sing" as we know it today. But it took over a century for the carol to acquire the melody with which we are now familiar. In 1840, Felix Mendelssohn composed *Festgesang*, a cantata celebrating Gutenberg's invention of the printing press. In 1885, William H. Cummings, organist at Waltham Abbey, England, fit it to the lyrics of "Hark! The Herald Angels Sing":

> Hark! the herald angels sing:
> Glory to the newborn King!

Peace on earth and mercy mild
God and sinners reconciled!
Joyful, all ye nations rise
Join the triumph of the skies.
With the angelic host proclaim:
Christ is born in Bethlehem!
Hark! the herald angels sing:
Glory to the newborn King!"

IN DULCI JUBILO

Besides the Advent hymn "O Come, O Come Emmanuel" (below) this carol is the oldest on our list and, along with "Ding Dong! Merrily on High" and "Angels We Have Heard on High," one of the three macaronic Christmas carols that we mention. "In Dulci Jubilo" is the most macaronic of the three, consistently alternating between English and Latin:

> *In dulci jubilo* [In sweet song]
> Let us our homage shew:
> Our heart's joy reclineth
> *In praesepio*; [In the manger]
> And like a bright star shineth
> *Matris in gremio.* [In his mother's lap]
> *Alpha es et O!* [You are the Alpha and Omega!]

The carol, which was originally in German and Latin,

is attributed to Blessed Henry Suso, a fourteenth-century Dominican friar, priest, and mystic. According to the story, when Suso was young he had a vision of angels who told him to cast aside all sorrow and join them in a dance. When he agreed, they drew him by the hand into the dance, and he began to sing "In Dulci Jubilo." Suso was a prolific author in both Latin and Middle High German, so it makes sense that he was thinking in both languages.

The song was influential on later composers. Johann Sebastian Bach adapted it several times: in BWV 368, 608, 703, 724, 729, and 751 (assuming it is his). BWV 729 is now the first organ voluntary at the end of Cambridge's Festival of Nine Lessons and Carols (see Chapter Twelve). Franz Liszt also uses the carol in his piano suite *Weihnachstbaum* ("Christmas Tree").

The composer Robert Lucas de Pearsall translated the German parts into English in 1837 and added a popular polyphonic arrangement. All-English versions include John Mason Neale's "Good Christian Men, Rejoice" and Arthur T. Russell's "Now Sing We, Now Rejoice."

IN THE BLEAK MID-WINTER

Christina Rosetti, sister of artist and poet Dante Gabriel Rosetti, was a well-regarded English poet of the Romantic era. In 1872, *Scribner's Magazine* published a request for a Christmas poem, and "In the Bleak

Mid-Winter" was Rosetti's response. In 1906, Gustav Holst set the poem to music. The first verse is:

> In the bleak midwinter, frosty wind made moan,
> Earth stood hard as iron, water like a stone;
> Snow had fallen, snow on snow, snow on snow,
> In the bleak midwinter, long ago.

IT CAME UPON THE MIDNIGHT CLEAR

Edmund H. Sears was an unusual man. Although an ordained Unitarian minister serving a church in Wayland, Massachusetts, he preached and believed in the divinity of Jesus Christ. In 1849, while suffering from personal melancholy and anxiety about war in Europe and the recent Mexican-American War, he obliged the request of a fellow pastor and composed a Christmas carol. You can hear the cry of pain about the plight of man in Sears's lyrics (which never actually mention the birth of Christ in Bethlehem) in verses such as:

> Yet with the woes of sin and strife
> The world has suffered long;
> Beneath the angel-strain have rolled
> Two thousand years of wrong;
> And man, at war with man, hears not

The love-song which they bring;
O hush the noise, ye men of strife,
And hear the angels sing.

A year later, Richard Storrs Willis wrote the melody "Carol." Willis trained under the great classical composer Felix Mendelssohn, and his tune is the one most Americans associate with "It Came upon a Midnight Clear." In the UK, however, a melody composed by Sir Arthur Sullivan in 1874 is more popular. The first verse is:

It came upon the midnight clear,
That glorious song of old,
From angels bending near the earth,
To touch their harps of gold:
"Peace on the earth, goodwill to men,
From heaven's all-gracious King."
The world in solemn stillness lay,
To hear the angels sing.

JINGLE BELLS

One of the best-known Christmas carols in English makes no mention of Christmas, and that is because it was never intended to be a Christmas carol. James Lord Pierpont (1822–1893) had a momentous life. The son of a Unitarian minister in Boston whose family traced their roots back to Charlemagne, he ran away to sea at the age of fourteen and sailed to California. Among his many occupations were: owner of a store during the California Gold Rush that burned to the ground, company clerk for the Fifth Georgia Cavalry during the Civil War, organist in a Presbyterian church, and head of the Musical Department at the Quitman Academy in Florida. In 1857, Pierpont was living in Savannah, Georgia (where he had followed his brother, the Unitarian minister John Pierpont Jr.), when he published a song called "One Horse Open Sleigh." Two years later, he published it again under the title "Jingle Bells."

Savannah, Georgia, and Medford, Massachusetts, vie for the honor of being home to this popular song. According to one theory, Pierpont wrote it in a local tavern while visiting his home state and then published it in Georgia. According to another, he wrote it in Savannah, maybe when he was feeling homesick for a New England winter and the one-mile sleigh races from Medford Square to Malden Square that he competed in as a boy. Still another theory claims that Pierpont wrote it for his father's Sunday School program held after Thanksgiving and that it was so popular the children sang it again at Christmas, where it stuck. The problem with this latter explanation is that some of the lyrics about courting were a bit too cheeky for children in a nineteenth-century Sunday school:

Now the ground is white

Go it while you're young,
Take the girls tonight
And sing this sleighing song.

As one commentator opined, "Fast sleighs and pretty girls. Some things never change."[3]

"Jingle Bells" was not a great financial success for Pierpont, although he did live long enough to see it become the first Christmas song ever recorded, in 1889, by Will Lyle on an Edison cylinder. "Jingle Bells" is also the first song, Christmas or otherwise, ever performed from outer space. On December 16, 1965, astronauts Wally Schirra and Tom Stafford in the Gemini VI reported to Mission Control a strange object going from north to south in a polar orbit that looked like a command module with eight smaller modules in front. The pilot of the command module, they continued, was wearing a red suit. Schirra and Stafford then broke into a performance of "Jingle Bells" with a tiny harmonica and five miniature sleigh bells that they had smuggled aboard. Those instruments are now displayed in the Smithsonian National Air and Space Museum as the first musical instruments played in space.

As for Pierpont, he was posthumously voted into the Songwriters Hall of Fame. We assume that it was for "Jingle Bells" and not for the ditties that this Yankee transplant wrote during the Civil War on behalf of the

Confederacy, including "Our Battle Flag," "Strike for the South," and "We Conquer or Die!"

JOY TO THE WORLD

Isaac Watts, the "Godfather of English Hymnody," wrote approximately 750 hymns, and one of them is "Joy to the World." It is said that Watts was inspired by three different scriptural passages: the second half of Psalm 98 ("Let the hills be joyful...for He cometh to judge the earth"), Psalm 96:11–12 ("Let the heavens rejoice and the earth be glad...."), and Genesis 3:17–18 (when God curses the land with thorns and thistles). The song is distinctive insofar as it celebrates Christ's triumphant Second Coming rather than His birth in Bethlehem. And with the lyric "Let every heart prepare him room" it also encourages the third coming remembered at Christmas (see Chapter Twelve).

Watts did not do much with the melody when he published his hymn in 1719, and so in 1839 Lowell Mason of Medfield, Massachusetts, composed a tune that borrowed several components from Handel's *Messiah*. In the late twentieth century, "Joy to the World" was designated the most-published Christmas hymn in North America:

> Joy to the world! the Lord is come;
> Let earth receive her King;
> Let every heart prepare him room,

And heaven and nature sing,
And heaven and nature sing,
And heaven, and heaven, and nature sing.

LITTLE DRUMMER BOY

"The Carol of the Drum" was the original name of this now-familiar Christmas song. It stands out in our list of carols because it is one of the few we know to have been written by a woman. Katherine Kennicott Davis was an American classical composer and teacher. In 1941, she was trying to take a nap but could not because of a song that was in her head. "Patapan" is a French Christmas carol about shepherds playing their instruments for the Infant Jesus. The title is onomatopoeic, meant to imitate the sound of a drum. In her drowsiness Davis converted the "patapan" to "pa rum pum pum-pum," which gave it a new rhythm. The result was "The Little Drummer Boy." Originally, the carol was for an a capella chorus, with the soprano singing the melody, the alto providing harmony, and the tenor and bass making the drum sounds.

The Trapp Family Singers (of *Sound of Music* fame) loved the song and recorded it in 1951, but it did not become a hit until the Jack Halloran Singers recorded it in 1957 with a different arrangement, one that is still used today. The first verse is:

Come, they told me

Pa rum pum pum-pum
A newborn King to see
Pa rum pum pum-pum
Our finest gifts we bring
Pa rum pum pum-pum
To lay before the King
Pa rum pum pum-pum
Rum pum pum-pum
Rum pum pum-pum
So to honor Him
Pa rum pum pum-pum
When we come.

LO, HOW A ROSE E'ER BLOOMING

No one knows who wrote this serene hymn, but it was in print as early as 1599 under its original German title, "Es ist ein Ros entsprungen," and it has more or less kept the same tune since 1609 thanks to German composer Michael Praetorius. The song is popular during Advent because it focuses on the Blessed Virgin Mary and her role in fulfilling the prophecies of Isaiah 11:1. (Mary is the tender rose sprouting from the tree of Jesse, preparing the way for the Messiah). There are several English translations, but the most popular is Theodore Baker's from 1894. Interestingly, although Marian devotion is usually associated with Catholicism, Protestant musicians have played a key role in the hymn's development: Praetorius, the son of a Lutheran minister, was a pioneer of

Protestant hymnody, and Baker's version first appeared in the *Psalter Hymnal* of the Christian Reformed Church in North America and *The United Methodist Hymnal*. The hymn continues to be recorded by modern artists, such as Linda Ronstadt and Sting. The first verse of Baker's translation is:

> Lo, how a rose e'er blooming,
> From tender stem hath sprung.
> Of Jesse's lineage coming,
> As men of old have sung;
> It came, a flow'ret bright,
> Amid the cold of winter,
> When half spent was the night.

O COME, ALL YE FAITHFUL

Nobody knows who wrote the Latin Christmas carol "Adeste, Fideles." It has at various times been attributed to St. Bonaventure (1221–1274), King John IV of Portugal (1604–1656), and the English composers John Reading (1645–1692) and John Francis Wade (1711–1786). Nor is the composer of the melody known. Was it Marcos Portugal, King John IV of Portugal, John Reading or his son of the same name, John Francis Wade, German Baroque composer George Frideric Handel, or Austrian opera composer Christoph Willibald Gluck? We do know that the most famous English translation was by Dr. Frederick Oakeley in 1841. Oakeley was an Anglican minister who was a part of the Oxford Movement (an attempt to reincorporate Catholic elements into the Church of England—among them, Latin hymns). In 1845, he was suspended by his superiors until he renounced his Romish opinions. Oakeley instead converted to Catholicism and was eventually ordained a priest. The first verse of Oakley's translation is:

> O come, all ye faithful, joyful, and triumphant!
> O come ye, O come ye to Bethlehem;
> Come and behold him
> Born the King of Angels:
> O come, let us adore Him,
> O come, let us adore Him,
> O come, let us adore Him,
> Christ the Lord.

O COME, O COME, EMMANUEL

We discussed the "secret code" in this popular Advent and Christmas hymn in Chapter Two. The Latin original, "Veni, Emmanuel," is from the twelfth century, and the English version we have today is thanks to an 1861 translation by John Mason Neale. Before the mid-nineteenth century, there was no melody definitively associated with the lyrics. But in 1851, Thomas Helmore took a medieval chant (probably one used for burial processions) and paired it with an early version of Neale's translation. It was a perfect fit, and today the tune is used for both the English and Latin versions, as if it had always been that way. The first verse of Neale's 1861 translation is:

> O come, O come, Emmanuel,
> And ransom captive Israel,
> That mourns in lonely exile here,
> Until the Son of God appear.
> Rejoice! Rejoice! Emmanuel
> Shall come to thee, O Israel.

O HOLY NIGHT

The parish priest of Roquemaure, France, was a happy man: the tricky business of renovating the church's organ was over and it had proven to be a success. The priest turned to a native of the town, a wineseller by the name of Placide Cappeau, and asked him to write a festive poem celebrating the completion of the project. A wine merchant might sound like an unusual choice for this commission, but Cappeau was no ordinary merchant. At the age of eight, a friend playing with a gun had accidentally shot his hand, causing so much damage that it had to be amputated. In atonement, the friend's father paid half of Cappeau's tuition for a fine liberal arts education. Cappeau had a license to practice law and maintained his father's wine business, but his first love was literature.

Cappeau responded to the priest's request in 1847 by composing "Minuit, Chrétiens" (Midnight, Christians).

He then asked his friend Adolphe Charles Adam, a professor at the Paris Conservatory of Music, to write a melody for it. Adams called the tune that he created "the religious Marseillaise" because he felt that it matched the republican, somewhat socialist verses of Cappeau's poem. On the other side of the Atlantic, the new song had appealed to abolitionists in the United States—particularly lines such as:

> Chains shall He break, for the slave is our brother
> And in His name, all oppression shall cease.

As a result, Unitarian minister and abolitionist John Sullivan Dwight translated "Minuit, Chrétiens" into English in 1855 under the title "O Holy Night." The carol became a hit, especially in the North.

The French original premiered in Roquemaure in 1847 with a performance by the opera singer Emily Laurey and—later pop singers' renditions notwithstanding—"O Holy Night" has found a home among classical musicians ever since. In modern times, the most popular classical recordings are by the well-loved tenors Luciano Pavarotti and Placido Domingo:

> O Holy night! The stars are brightly shining,
> It is the night of our dear Savior's birth;

Long lay the world in sin and error pining,
'Til He appeared and the soul felt its worth.
A thrill of hope the weary world rejoices
For yonder breaks a new and glorious
    morn;
Fall on your knees, oh hear the Angel
    voices!
O night divine, O night when Christ was
    born,
O night, O Holy night, O night divine!

O LITTLE TOWN OF BETHLEHEM

Phillips Brooks, the rector of the Episcopal Church of the Holy Trinity in Philadelphia, toured the Holy Land in 1865. Three years later, inspired by his visit to the birthplace of the Infant Jesus, he wrote "O Little Town of Bethlehem" for his church's Christmas Sunday School service. The original carol had four verses, the last one being:

Where children pure and happy
Pray to the Blessed Child:
Where misery cries out to Thee
Son of the Undefiled;
Where Charity stands watching
And Faith holds wide the door,
The dark night wakes the glory hearts
And Christmas comes once more.

The line "Son of the Undefiled" led to some light-hearted ribbing from Brooks's colleagues that it smacked of the doctrine of the Immaculate Conception of the Blessed Virgin Mary, a no-no for most Protestants. Brooks changed the line to "Son of the Mother mild," and eventually decided to drop the entire verse.

Brooks asked the parish organist, Louis H. Redner, to set his words to music. Working on short notice and under great pressure, Redner could not come up with any ideas until the night before the children's choir was to have their first practice of the new carol. Roused late at night by "an angel-strain whispering in [his] ear," he seized a piece of paper and wrote down the treble of the tune. Redner then went back to bed and filled in the harmony in the morning before heading off to church.[4] Neither he nor Brooks ever dreamed that the song would last beyond that one performance.

Redner's tune, later dubbed "St. Louis," is the one that most Americans know, but in the UK and the Commonwealth the carol is sung to "Forest Green," an adaptation of the English folk ballad "The Ploughboy's Dream" by Ralph Vaughn Williams.

As a hymn, "O Little Town of Bethlehem" is unusual in that it is more of a meditation than a prayer to God:

> O little town of Bethlehem,
> How still we see thee lie!
> Above thy deep and dreamless sleep

The silent stars go by.
Yet in thy dark streets shineth
The everlasting light;
The hopes and fears of all the years
Are met in thee tonight.

ONCE IN ROYAL DAVID'S CITY

Cecil Frances Alexander was a talented Anglo-Irish hymnwriter who, under the influence of the Oxford Movement, had a bright idea: teach the Apostles' Creed through song. In 1848, she published an anthology entitled *Hymns for Little Children* comprising a different hymn for each article of the Creed. To illuminate the meaning of "Born of a Virgin Mary," Alexander wrote "Once in Royal David's City."

Hymns for Little Children was an enormous success: by the end of the nineteenth century it had gone through sixty editions. There was only one problem: its hymns were not hymns but poems since Alexander had not included sheet music. A year later, however, London organist Henry John Gauntlett discovered the book and put "Once in Royal David's City" to music. Gauntlett is the author of over a thousand hymn tunes, but this one, called "Irby," is his most famous. Since 1919, the song has been the processional hymn for the Festival of Nine Lessons and Carols at King's College, Cambridge (see Chapter Twelve). The first verse is:

Once in royal David's city
Stood a lowly cattle shed,
Where a mother laid her Baby
In a manger for His bed:
Mary was that mother mild,
Jesus Christ her little Child.

RUDOLPH, THE RED-NOSED REINDEER

Santa Claus originally had only eight tiny reindeer pulling his sleigh, but that changed in 1939 thanks to the success of a Montgomery Ward Department Store children's book written by Robert L. May. May, a copyeditor for the company, had been commissioned to write "an animal story with a character like Ferdinand the Bull," and so he chose a reindeer and made him an outsider in order to reflect May's own "painfully shy childhood." Despite his boss's initial reservations, the story was a great success, especially after cowboy singer Gene Autry sang it in 1949 and made it the second best-selling Christmas song of all time ("White Christmas" is the first). May enjoyed enormous financial success but not for long: since the top U.S. individual income tax rate at the time was 92 percent, the government took almost all his wealth, and within seven years of quitting his job at Montgomery Ward he was back at his old desk. But Rudolph's creator took it in good stride. Towards the end of his life he wrote: "Today children all over the world read and hear about the little deer who started out in life as a loser, just as I did. But they learn that when he gave himself for others, his handicap became the very means through which he achieved happiness. My reward is knowing that every year, when Christmas rolls around, Rudolf still brings that message to millions, both young and old."[5]

Incidentally, although he later converted to Catholicism, May was Jewish when he wrote "Rudolph." So was May's brother-in-law Johnny Marks, who wrote the music for "Rudolph" and went on to write such other hits as "Holly Jolly Christmas," "Rockin' around the Christmas Tree," "Silver and Gold," and "Run Rudolph Run." So was Mel Tormé, author of "The Christmas Song." So was Irving Berlin, author of "White Christmas." So were Sammy Cahn and Jule Styne (born Samuel Cohen and Julius Stein), authors of "Let it Snow! Let it Snow! Let it Snow!" So were Edward Pola and George Wyle (born Sidney Edward Pollacsek and Bernard Weissman), the authors of "It's the Most Wonderful Time of the Year." So were Joan Javits and Philip Springer, authors of "Santa, Baby." And so were Jay Livingston (born Jacob Harold Levison) and Ray Evans, who wrote "Silver Bells."

SEE AMID THE WINTER'S SNOW

Edward Caswall, who relinquished his position as an Anglican minister, converted to Catholicism, and became an Oratorian priest under the influence of St. John Henry Newman, had a knack for translation: he rendered all of the Latin hymns from the Roman Breviary into English, including the well-known "Come, Holy Ghost." But Caswall's famous Christmas carol is his own. "See, amid the Winter's Snow," which ingeniously develops a dialogue between the singers and the shepherds who adored the Christ Child, was first published in 1858. In 1871, Sir John Goss, an organist at St. Paul's Cathedral and a professor at the Royal Academy of Music, wrote the tune "Humility" specifically for the carol and made several sagacious recommendations about its performance.

The first verse and chorus are:

> See amid the winter's snow,
> Born for us on earth below,
> See the tender Lamb appears,
> Promised from eternal years.
>
> Hail, thou ever-blessed morn!
> Hail, redemption's happy dawn!
> Sing through all Jerusalem,
> Christ is born in Bethlehem!

SILENT NIGHT

While "O Holy Night" would not have been written had an organ not been repaired, "Silent Night" would not have been written had an organ not failed to be repaired. And whereas "O Holy Night" would not have been written had a priest not requested it, "Silent Night" would not have been written had a priest not done it himself.

Father Joseph Mohr was the pastor of the Catholic church in Obendorf, Austria. On Christmas Eve 1818, he received some bad news: the organ, which had been damaged by a river flood, would not be ready for Midnight Mass, and thus the glorious High Mass he had planned for Christmas could not be celebrated. To offer his flock some consolation, Father Mohr dusted off a poem he had written in 1816, in the aftermath of the Napoleonic Wars, entitled "Stille Nacht, Heilige Nacht" ("Silent Night, Holy Night"). He then asked his friend Franz Gruber, a teacher and organist in a nearby village, for music to accompany it; within a few hours of receiving the lyrics, Gruber composed the now familiar tune.

The organ's repairman was impressed with the new hymn, and so he gave a copy to a family of singers called the Rainers. The family loved it and began singing it at their concerts wherever they went: Austria, Germany, and, from 1839 to 1843, America. "Silent Night" is now loved worldwide and, as of 2011, one of UNESCO's declared intangible cultural heritages.

History's most poignant performance of "Silent Night" occurred on the front lines of World War I during the so-called Christmas Truce. On Christmas Eve 1914, German soldiers put up Christmas trees on their parapets and began to sing "Stille Nacht." The astonished English troops cheered when it was over and then sang "Silent Night" in reply. Not long after, both sides ventured into No Man's Land, where they exchanged gifts of tobacco, food, buttons, and other souvenirs. Overall, 100,000 troops participated in what was in some respects the last gasp of the old Christian code of chivalry before it yielded to the modern doctrine of total war. There was a much smaller Christmas truce in 1915, but by 1916 all good will among the combatants had dried up in the face of the Great War's cruelty.

The first verse of the hymn is:

> Silent night, holy night!
> All is calm, all is bright.
> Round yon Virgin, Mother and Child.
> Holy infant so tender and mild,
> Sleep in heavenly peace,
> Sleep in heavenly peace.

WE THREE KINGS

See Chapter Thirteen.

WHAT CHILD IS THIS?

Like most businessmen, William Chatterton Dix did not get overworked by theological niceties or deep existential questions. But when this manager of an insurance office in Glasgow, Scotland, was struck down by a serious illness at the age of twenty-five, he experienced a spiritual renewal. As he slowly recovered from his near-death experience, Dix read the Bible extensively and then wrote hymns inspired by what he had read. "Alleluia! Sing to Jesus!" and "As with Gladness Men of Old," are still sung today. But Dix's most famous work is "The Manger Throne," better known to you and me as "What Child Is This?" The poem was written in 1865, and when it was finally published in 1871, it was set to the tune of "Greensleeves," a traditional English folk song. The carol, with its pensive and somewhat sorrowful mood, struck a chord in the hearts of Americans, who had recently undergone the trauma of the Civil War. To this day, the song is more popular in the United States than its native Great Britain. The first verse is:

> What Child is this who, laid to rest,
> On Mary's lap is sleeping?
> Whom Angels greet with anthems sweet,
> While shepherds watch are keeping?

Chapter Ten

WASSAIL! CHRISTMAS FOOD AND DRINK

hristmas would not be Christmas without its seasonal meats and treats. The traditional English observance of the holiday was so tied to breads, cakes, and meat pies that the Italians once had a phrase for being overwhelmed with work: *Ha più da fare che i forni di Natale in Inghilterra*— "He has more to do than the Christmas ovens in England."[1] But the English do not have a monopoly on Yuletide feasting. In Chapters Twelve and Thirteen we will survey some of the rich culinary traditions surrounding New Year's celebrations and

Epiphany; here we focus more on Christmas Eve and Christmas Day.

CHRISTMAS EVE

THE MEATLESS MEAL

For centuries, the Christmas Eve dinner was one of the most important family meals of the year; it was also a time to extend hospitality to those who had no families of their own. Steeped in ritual and expectation, the dinner straddled the fence between the penitence of Advent and the joy of Christmas. Because December 24 was a day of fasting and of abstaining from the meat of warm-blooded animals, it was long the custom to have a special seafood meal the night before Christmas.

In some parts of Italy, *Cenone* or Christmas Eve Supper usually consists of twelve courses in honor of the Apostles, but the content of those courses varies from region to region and family to family. In southern Italy, the meal is called the Feast of the Seven Fishes. One favorite is *capitone* or eel sauteed in onion and shallots; another is *fritto misto* or "mixed fry," deep-fried fish, vegetables, or fruit. Other courses of a traditional Italian Christmas Eve dinner can consist of pasta with a meatless sauce like gorgonzola or anchovy. In Abruzzi (in southern Italy), the feast includes *insalata de arance*, an orange salad made with orange slices and black pepper marinating in olive oil.

Portugal observes the meatless tradition with *bacalhau* or salt cod, although some regions prefer *polvo* or octopus, either with rice or roasted.

A traditional Mexican meal includes a "salad of the Good Night" (*ensalada de Nochebuena*), marinated fish (*seviche*), and fried cakes (*buñuelos*). Armenians have a simple meal of fried fish, lettuce, and boiled spinach—for according to legend, that was what Our Lady ate the night that Christ was born.

In Provence (southern France), the *Gros Souper* or Big Supper consists of *aioli*, a delicious garlic mayonnaise served with fish, snails, and vegetables. For dessert there are thirteen different treats: fruits, nuts, chocolates, and so forth. Thirteen is considered a lucky number in some places, for it is the sum of Christ and the Apostles. [2]

In Slavic lands, the Christmas Eve meal (*Wigilia* in Polish) cannot begin until the first star in the night sky is sighted; it is usually the responsibility of the youngest child to keep watch for it. Stalks of grain are placed in the four corners of the room for a bountiful harvest, and hay is spread out under the tablecloth in honor of the manger. In Poland, the meal begins with grace and the breaking of a rectangular Christmas wafer called *opłatek* ("offering"). The father breaks off a piece and passes the remainder to the rest of the family until everyone has a piece. As the wafer is passed around, prayers are said for loved ones. The ritual symbolizes the unity of the family in Christ as well forgiveness and reconciliation. In parts of Ukraine, a wheat porridge called *kutia* serves a similar function. The twelve-course meal in honor of the Apostles can consist of various soups such as borscht and fish like herring and carp: some Poles buy a live carp a couple of days earlier and let it swim around in their bathtub for maximum freshness. For dessert, they enjoy a compote made of twelve different fruits (again in honor of the Apostles).

BREADS AND CAKES

The prominence of wheat products on the Christmas table can be traced to the age before Christ, when the peoples of Europe used the period around the winter solstice to pray for a good crop in the upcoming year and to honor the deceased ancestors who had bequeathed them their fields. Symbolically significant breads and cakes were baked, and wheat was displayed around the home. With the spread of Christianity came a purging of pagan customs, but many of the old treats were retained or modified. Most countries have some sort of traditional Christmas cake baked on Christmas Eve and eaten during the season.

In Ireland, circular carraway seed cakes for each member of the household were so popular that the Gaelic name for Christmas Eve is *Oidhche na ceapairi*—the "Night of Cakes."

In some parts of Germany, cakes were adorned with a figure of the Christ Child made from sugar; today,

Christollen, a bread made with butter, sugar, almonds, and raisins, is popular.

In Slavic countries, white wafers blessed by the priest and eaten with syrup or honey are imprinted with scenes of the Nativity and distributed by the father during the Christmas Eve dinner as a symbol of love and peace. In Lithuania these are called "bread of the angels" and in Poland, as we saw above, *opłatki*. Lithuanians also have *kūčiukai* or Christmas cakes, small poppy-seed loaves that are served on Christmas Eve and left out overnight for deceased loved ones.

In France and French Canada, small round loaves (*pains d'habitant*) are baked for Christmastide. In southern France, the Christmas loaf (*pain calendeau*) is cut into four pieces and eaten only after the first quarter has been given to a poor person.

In Hungary, folks eagerly await a large rolled cake filled with poppy seeds and walnuts called *mákos és diós kalacs*.

The Greek *Christopsomo* (Christ bread) is a round loaf decorated with a cross of dough and agricultural symbols meant to invoke prosperity. It is eaten on Christmas Eve, although a loaf is sometimes left out in the hope that Christ Himself will come for it.

Vánočka is plaited bread similar to brioche that is enjoyed in the Czech Republic and Slovakia. It is traditionally made with three braids placed over one another that are said to represent the Infant Jesus wrapped in swaddling clothes. Slovenia, on the other hand, has a potato bread called *krompirjev kruh*, which is moist with a crusty outer layer.

In Italy, *panettone* and *pandoro* are the favored sweet breads for the season. Panettone, which means "luxury cake," has been around since the fifteen hundreds, and pandoro ("golden bread") was developed in the Middle Ages. Prior to developments in mass production, both were enjoyed only by the elite.

OTHER BREADY TREATS

Many Christmas desserts are substitutes or descendants of older Yuletide bread traditions. We already explained England's famous Christmas pudding in Chapter Two. Here are a few more highlights from around the world.

Germany can boast of several Christmas treats including: *Bethmännchen*, a marzipan pastry made with almond, powdered sugar, and rosewater; *Dominostein*, a multilayered sweet covered in dark chocolate; *Magenbrot*, a small sweet glazed biscuit; and *Rumtopf*, a mixture of fruit, rum, and sugar in a stoneware pot. *Spekulatius*, *Spritzgebäck*, and *Springerle* are different kinds of hard biscuit or cookie. The generic name for German Christmas cookies is *Weihnachtsplätzchen*.

Spain also has at least a dozen different Christmas delights, but the oldest and most famous of all is *polvorón*, a kind of shortbread invented in Seville in the sixteenth century by nuns. *Polvorón* remains a popular Christmas dessert in Spain and her former colonies, as does *turrón*, a nougat confection made with honey, sugar, egg, and toasted almonds. Also popular in Spain are *roscos de vino de Navidad* or Christmas wine donuts, made with olive oil, sweet muscat wine, and powdered sugar.

The oldest Christmas cookies in Scandinavia are pepper nuts (*pepper nodder* in Denmark and *peppernotter* in Sweden), which owe their existence to the medieval love of holiday spices. *Drommar* are light and airy cookies while *krumkake* are delicate, paper-thin wafers. *Sandbakelser* or sand tarts are Norwegian almond cookies baked in decorative molds. Also popular in northern countries are deep-fried treats such as Norway's *fattigmann* ("poor man's cakes"), Sweden and Norway's flower-shaped rosettes, and Denmark's delicious donut holes called *aebleskiver*, which are served to visitors between Christmas and New Year's Eve.

In Greece, *melomakarona* (honey cookies) and *kourabiedes* (sugar-coated butter cookies) take pride of place during Christmastime. Made from local ingredients such as oil, honey, oranges, and nuts (which are among Greece's most popular food products), they have been around since ancient times.

Potica is a delicious nut roll made of walnuts, sugar, tarragon, quark, hazelnut, and poppy seed. It is traditionally served in Slovenia during both Christmas and Easter. Romania enjoys a sweet bread called *cozonac*, while Bulgaria has *koledna pitka*, which contains a lucky silver coin.

Provence, France, enjoys a sweet bread made with floral water called *pompe de Noël* either as a Christmas Eve dessert or for Christmas breakfast. France and French Canada also make a rich cake of whole wheat, brown sugar, and dates called *carreaux aux dattes*.

Finland has *pulla*, a delicious flaky cardamom roll, and Norway has *julekake*, a cake made with cardamom, raisins, and candied citrons that goes well with butter and brown goat cheese.

Finally, the United States has the simple sugar cookie, cut into various holiday shapes and covered in icing or sprinkled with variously colored sugars.

GINGERBREAD

Two other breads deserve separate mention: gingerbread and fruitcake.

In antiquity and the Middle Ages, ginger was valued for its medicinal properties: it was used to treat flatulence, indigestion, and hangovers; and as a preservative. It was also popular, of course, as a food flavoring. Tradition credits an Armenian monk named St. Gregory of Nicopolis with teaching priests in Bondaroy, France, how to make gingerbread in A.D. 992. The confection became popular at festivals and fairs, and over time it became associated with Christmas markets and celebrations. Today almost every European country has its own version of gingerbread. Gingerbread men are said to have been invented by Queen Elizabeth I of England, who made them resemble important foreign dignitaries. German *Lebkuchen* are honey-sweetened gingerbread cookies; Nuremburg, the "Gingerbread Capital of the World," has been making them since 1395. In the Nordic countries, folks enjoy *pepperkaker* (Norway), *pepparkakor* (Sweden), *brunkager* (Denmark), *piparkökur* (Iceland), *piparkakut* (Finland), *piparkoogid* (Estonia), and *piparkūkas* (Latvia). Poland has a Torún gingerbread that has been made in that city since the thirteenth century as well as other regional variations. *Perník* is a popular gingerbread biscuit in the Czech Republic at Christmas. Cut into different shapes (hearts, stars, and animals), it is also used as a Christmas tree decoration.

As for the gingerbread house, it may have begun as a marketing gimmick to attract customers at Christmas markets. Another theory is that it was inspired by the witch's house in the Grimm Brothers' fairy tale "Hansel and Gretel": to this day, the German word for gingerbread houses is *Hexenhäusle* or "witches' houses." But pious legend, as always, has the most charming explanation. Apparently there was a fourth Wise Man who fell ill as he was following the Christmas star and was taken in by a kindly rabbi in Syria. The rabbi told his guest that he had his students make houses of bread as a way of sustaining their hope in the Messiah, who would be born in Bethlehem (Hebrew for "house of bread"). The Wise Man gave the rabbi his chest full of ginger roots (which he had planned on giving to the Infant Jesus) and suggested that he and his students add ground ginger to their houses for flavor and as a preservative.

Whatever the origins, the gingerbread house is a cherished tradition in many countries. In Scandinavia, the *pepparkakorhus* is the centerpiece of the table and often a family project. In 2013 the Texas A&M Traditions Club in Bryan, Texas, built the world's largest gingerbread house. The completely edible edifice was a full-sized (39,000 cubic feet) house capacious enough for a family of five. The club sold tickets for a tour (and a chance to meet Santa Claus) and donated the proceeds to the nearby St. Joseph's Hospital.[3]

FRUITCAKE

Fruitcake has been around since Biblical times: Abigail, for instance, brought King David "two hundred cakes of pressed figs" (1 Samuel 25:18), and given fruitcake's notoriously long shelf life, perhaps one of those cakes is still out there. In the Middle Ages, fruitcakes were for festive occasions such as weddings and Christmas. Many cultures enjoy them year-round, but some associate them especially with Christmas and Epiphany. Poland has its *keks*, Portgual *bolo Rei*, Romania *cozonac*, and Chile *pan de Pascua*. Germany has several versions of *stollen*, which we described in the "Breads and Cakes" section above (there is a thin line between fruitcake and sweet bread).

The United Kingdom has a wide assortment of regional fruitcakes that range from light to moist and rich. They are typically covered in marzipan, icing, and decorations such as holly, snowmen, or robins. England's tastes rubbed off onto most of the Commonwealth countries such as Canada, New Zealand, and India, all of which enjoy fruitcake at Christmas. In the English-speaking Caribbean, "black cake" is made with mixed fruits, rum, and wine and given as a gift between Christmas and New Year's. Black cake can be prepared months ahead of time and is more closely related to the English Christmas pudding than anything else.

In the United States, mail-order fruitcakes from companies such as Collin Street Bakery in Corsicana, Texas, and The Claxton Bakery in Claxton, Georgia, are a popular option. Because these are Southern producers with easy access to nuts, American fruitcakes are typically rich in this ingredient—hence the expression "nuttier than a fruitcake." The mass production of fruitcakes, combined with their longevity, has led to this traditional treat's being the butt of many a joke. Johnny Carson liked to quip that there was only one fruitcake in the world that was passed from family to family. Manito Springs, Colorado, hosts a Great Fruitcake Toss every January in which contestants toss small fruitcakes or devise contraptions such as air cannons to hurl an old fruitcake through the air. Categories include distance, speed, accuracy, and balance. Fruitcakes can be brought from home for the event, but the organizers also make preservative-free fruitcakes that, after they have served their purpose, go to a pig named Jezebel.

CANDY CANES

No one is certain when or why candy canes came about, but one of the more plausible stories is that they were invented in 1670 by the choirmaster of Cologne Cathedral in Germany as a way of keeping his young singers quiet during a long Christmas pageant.[4] The clever elder made a hard candy resembling a shepherd's crook, and because of the shape, the treat eventually became an easy and popular way to decorate the Christmas tree. Later, pious imagination would ascribe other qualities to the candy cane. Its shape was said to resemble the "J" in Jesus, the red stripe His Blood, and the white either His purity or the minty Biblical herb hyssop (which was used at the Crucifixion).

CHESTNUTS

1946 was the year that Nat King Cole first sang the iconic words penned by Robert Wells and Mel Tormé: "Chestnuts roasting on an open fire." For Americans at the time, the distinctive aroma of roasting chestnuts was a familiar part of Christmases past. But already by

1946, the delicious holiday treat was sadly becoming a distant memory.

The American chestnut tree (*Castanea dentata*) reaches heights of a hundred feet and produces acorn-sized nuts in late autumn. A source of food and furniture for centuries, the majestic trees could once be seen from Maine to the Mississippi and from the Appalachians to the Ohio Valley. It is estimated that in 1900 there were four billion chestnut trees in North America, which was almost half the trees in the forests on the East Coast.

Then, in 1904, a gardener at the New York Zoological Park noticed that a chestnut tree was afflicted with a strange blight. An Asian chestnut tree planted in Long Island had brought with it a deadly disease to which its American cousin was especially susceptible. Within forty years, nearly all four billion American chestnuts were dead. Today *Castanea dentata* is listed as a critically endangered species and mostly survives outside its historic range, where the blight is less virulent. Chinese and European chestnuts are still available for consumption, but they are a pale imitation of their American native. Whereas the American chestnut tastes like a carrot raw and like candy when cooked, the other chestnuts are as bland as a potato, better for stuffing than for snacking. Fortunately, scientists are working on cross-breeding the American chestnut tree with the Chinese, which is highly resistant to blight. Some day in the future there may be a return to the smells and tastes of the past.

CHRISTMAS DAY

RÉVEILLON MEAL

Réveillon, which comes from the French word, "to awaken," is used to denote Christmas Eve and also the meal held in the wee hours after returning from Midnight Mass. Great French foods such as *boudin* (blood sausage), oysters, and roast turkey grace the table, while in French Canada there is a delicious meat pie called *tourtière* and a green ketchup called "chow chow." The dinner is traditionally concluded with a pastry called a *bûche de Noël* (Christmas log).

THE MAIN COURSE

Christmas dinner at the Cratchits.
Philip V. Allingham

The Feast of the Nativity calls for great feasting at the table. The traditional Christmas Day dinner varies according to nationality, but it is generally marked by hearty and delicious dishes.

The English have preserved the medieval tradition of eating goose and plum pudding, but by the time Dickens wrote a *Christmas Carol* in 1844, they had also adopted the American custom of roast turkey.

Both goose and turkey are popular in many parts of continental Europe, while the Scandinavians prefer some kind of pork, such as ham or spareribs. That goes for Icelanders, too, but they also like ptarmigan, a game bird similar to grouse.

The main dish in Greece is roast turkey, but with a Mediterranean twist: it is stuffed with rice and chestnuts.

Germans enjoy goose, rabbit, duck, *Krustenbraten* (crispy pork roast), potato dumplings, and sausage stuffing. Jamaicans, on the other hand, prefer curried goat, while New Zealanders like lamb roasted or barbecued in an underground pit.

MINCE PIE

And then there is mince pie, the sweet dessert that began as a savory meat dish. During the Middle Ages it was popular in the Middle East to mix meat, fruit, and spices. Crusaders brought this technique back with them, and before long mincemeat pies were all the rage. Early recipes called for beef tongue, chicken, eggs, raisins, orange and lemon peel, sugar, and spices such as cinnamon, cloves, and nutmeg. But cooks were versatile, using whatever was available. That could include wild game such as venison and, on one memorable occasion, whale: For Christmas in 1861, James Swan prepared a mincemeat pie from a piece of whale meat given to him by the Makah Indians in what is now Washington State. Swan's fears about how his concoction would be received were allayed when his guests devoured the first serving and asked for more.⁵

Because of their expense, mincemeat pies were only eaten on special occasions, and as the "Christmas pie" they had a special significance. The ingredients were seen as a symbol of the Magis' gifts to the Infant Jesus, and the pies were baked in a large, oblong shape to represent the manger in Bethlehem. (Such pies tend to sink in the middle, creating a manger-like appearance.) Sometimes a figure of the Infant Jesus was placed on top. At dinner, the "baby" was removed and the "manger" was eaten. The Puritans were not happy with this devotion, and when they came to power in the seventeenth century, they condemned the practice as idolatrous (see Chapter One). The mincemeat pie survived the persecution but only by changing to its now familiar circular shape.

During the Victorian era, the pie became smaller, sweeter, and less carnal. Today's mince pies contain no meat (although they are still made with animal products such as suet) and are roughly the size of a cookie.

CHRISTMAS DRINKS

Christmas celebrations have long been associated with drinking, which is one of the reasons that the Puritans despised the holiday. Wine is an essential part of the Christmas dinner in Mediterranean countries, while northern European nations typically enjoy beer and ale;

indeed, for centuries they have made special brews for the occasion. Christmas beer or ale is defined as a seasonal beverage available only during Christmastime. It is usually strong in alcohol and includes "Christmas-y" ingredients like orange, cloves, vanilla, and cinnamon.

Here are some more signature Yuletide libations.

MULLED DRINKS

Winter is the perfect time for something mulled—that is, a drink that has been heated and to which sugar, spices, and fruits have been added.[6]

In German-speaking countries, *glühwein* or "glow wine" (from the hot pokers once used to warm it) is a traditional holiday favorite that consists of red wine, sugar, oranges, lemons, and spices such as cinnamon, star anise, cloves, and vanilla. One variation with great visual appeal is *feuerzangenbowle* or "fire punch." Mulled wine without sugar is placed in a metal bowl. A sugar loaf soaked in rum is then placed on a bridge stretching over the bowl and set alight. The sugar loaf is enveloped in a blue flame and slowly melts into the bowl.

In Scandinavia, *glögg* (Swedish and Icelandic) or *gløgg* (Norwegian and Danish) is the key Christmas beverage. The common ingredients are red wine, sugar, and spices such as cardamom, ginger, cinnamon, cloves, and bitter orange, but each nation has its own distinctive approach. In Sweden, the drink is served with a spoon to scoop out the fruits and nuts; in Norway, the wine is spiked with a shot of aquavit; and in Denmark, it is fortified with port.

In England, a "wassail" was originally a toast. The Old English *wæs hail* means "Be in [good] health!" and the proper response is *drinc hail* or "Drink [good] health!" Eventually, the word's meaning migrated to what was being drunk. The first wassails were mulled ales served in large multi-handled communal bowls and featuring ingredients such as roasted apples, eggs, sugar, nutmeg, cloves, and ginger. Later on, hot cider became the more common base.

One popular wassail is Lamb's Wool. The curious name is probably due to the fuzzy appearance of the peeled and roasted apples, but it is also a nice tie-in to the Lamb of God, who is the reason for the season. Lamb's Wool can be made with ale, cider, or both, and there is even a nice little ditty to remind you of the other ingredients:

> Next crowne the bowle full of
> With gentle Lambs wooll,
> Adde sugar, nutmeg, and ginger,
> With store of ale too,
> And thus ye must doe
> To make the Wassaile a swinger.[7]

And if, where you are, the weather at Christmastime is too hot for something mulled, do what tropical Jamaica does. Sorrel Punch is a tart, dark red punch served cold that consists of red wine, white rum, and hibiscus (sorrel) tea brewed with ginger, pimento, cinnamon, and other spices.

DAIRY DRINKS

Besides the fruit of the vine, Christmas imbibers turn to the dairy for something in their glass. Perhaps the original idea behind consuming these calorie-rich drinks was to pack on an extra layer of insulation during the cold winter months (which would subsequently be lost during the Great Fast of Lent).

Eggnog has been a popular Christmas drink in the English-speaking world for at least two hundred years. Made with milk, cream, eggs, and sugar and sprinkled with nutmeg, it can be served without alcohol or with brandy, rum, whiskey, or bourbon, and it can be served cold or warm. The name eggnog may come from the warm version: according to one theory, the "nogg" in "eggnog" is a variation of the Scottish term "nugg," which means "ale warmed with a poker." The Scots themselves, however, prefer their own Auld Man's Milk, made with eggs, sugar, and scotch. Named after Robert Burns's "Auld Lang Syne," it is especially popular at their New Year's Eve blowout known as Hogmanay (see Chapter Twelve).

The Tom and Jerry is a variation of eggnog that is always served hot. Now a classic Christmastide mixed drink, it was invented as a promotional product. Pierce Egan came up with it in the 1820s to promote his book and play about two friends named Tom and Jerry, and we suspect that the drink, in turn, was the inspiration behind the names of the famous cartoon cat-and-mouse duo from the 1940s. To go from friends to a drink to frenemies is perhaps an appropriate journey, at least if the friends drink too much.

Germany's version of eggnog is called *eierlikör*. Its claim to fame is that it is thick enough to eat with a spoon, which is why it is diluted with a sweet white wine like a Riesling and some rum, brandy, or whiskey.

Dutch *advocaat* is an egg-based liqueur similar in flavor to *eierlikör*. According to legend, a distiller was trying to duplicate a drink that Dutch colonists were enjoying in Brazil. The original recipe included avocados as a thickening agent (hence the name), but the distiller used the more easily obtainable egg.

Lithuania's *aguonų pienas*—"poppyseed milk"— does not contain milk, but we might as well talk about it here. Poppy seeds are soaked in hot water overnight before being crushed or "milked." Cool water, honey, and *viryta* (a potent spiced honey liqueur) are then added.

In Venezuela, *ponche crema* has been produced commercially since 1900. The cream-based liqueur is a holiday drink served cold in small cups as an aperitif. Cuba, on the other hand, prefers *crema de vie*, made with condensed or evaporated milk, vanilla extract, sugar, egg yolks, white rum, and a sprinkle or stick of cinnamon.

Rompope is a vanilla liqueur made from egg yolk, sugar, milk, cinnamon, and alcohol. Named after the Spanish version of eggnog (*rompon*), the beverage was invented by nuns from the Santa Clara Convent in Puebla, Mexico. According to one story, the nuns wanted something to serve their guests; according to another, they had used hundreds of egg whites to shellac some newly painted sacred images in their church and wanted to put the yolks to good use (which they certainly did). Whatever the reason, the drink was a success. Rompope is enjoyed year round in Mexico and throughout Central America, but it is especially associated with the Christmas season.

For a lighter touch, tropical Puerto Rico has *coquito* or "little coconut." The holiday drink is made from coconut milk, coconut cream, sweetened condensed milk, and rum or *pitorro*, the local moonshine.

In Chile, *cola de mono* or "monkey's tail" is made with coffee, sugar, milk, cloves, and *aguardiente*, a sweet sugar-cane alcohol. A favorite at Chilean Christmas parties, it is said to have been invented in the 1900s by a clever fellow after the wine ran out at a party. (Not exactly the miracle at the Wedding of Cana, but we'll take it.) Ecuador, on the other hand, uses aguardiente to make *canelazo*, a hot drink that also includes cinnamon sticks, boiled water, passionfruit juice, and lemon juice.

Chapter Eleven

LOOKING A LOT LIKE CHRISTMAS: OTHER CHRISTMAS CUSTOMS OLD AND NEW

Christmas is built upon a beautiful and intentional paradox; that the birth of the homeless should be celebrated in every home.

—G. K. Chesterton[1]

By the early twentieth century, G. K. Chesterton was able to observe that Christmas had become a hectic time. "People have to rush about for a few weeks," he wrote, "if it is only to stay at home for a few hours."[2] And during those few hours, they were often bored without some external diversion (and this was before smart phones!). Most moderns cannot amuse themselves, he observed, because they are too used to being amused.

But back in the days when the weather drove families indoors and onto their own resources, they rose to the occasion and invented their own amusements and celebrations, customs that we still observe today. Having already looked at Christmas in song and food, let us turn in this chapter to some other cherished traditions, including some homey practices that honor the Homeless One. Let's start with the many names for the holiday.

NAMES

Most languages take their name for Christmas from the occasion for the feast: the birth of Jesus Christ. Hence *Genethlia* in Greek, *Karácsony* in Hungarian, *Boze Narodzenie* in Polish (all of which mean God's Birth), and *Rozhudestvo Khrista* (Christ's Birth) in Russian and Ukrainian. Names in several languages are derived from the Latin for Christ's birth (*nativitas* or *dies natalis*), such as the Italian *Il Natale*, the Spanish *La Navidad*, the Portuguese *Natal*, the southern French *Nadal*, and the Welsh *Nadolig*.

Four interesting outliers are French, German, the Scandinavian languages, and English. As we have seen, the French *Noël* (Cornish *Nowell*) means "news." Thus the Angel announces in an old English carol:

I come from hevin to tell

The best nowellis that ever befell.[3]

The German *Weinacht*, on the other hand, means "blessed or holy night." (Czech and Slovak follow a similar pattern.)

Scandinavian nations, on the other hand, have different forms of our "Yule" as the principal name for the feast: *Jul* in Danish, Norwegian, and Swedish; *Jol* in Icelandic, and *Joulua* in Finnish. *Jul* may be from the Old Germanic word *Jol* for a turning of the wheel—that is, the orbit of the sun after the winter solstice—or it may be from *geol*, the Anglo-Saxon word for a feast. Since the period around the winter solstice was a great time of feasting, December was known as *geola*: feast month.

And then there is the English "Christmas," or "Christ's Mass," which puts before us the specific worship offered in honor of Christ's birth. Before the Reformation, the English liked to name their feasts after the Mass celebrated on that day: Michaelmas for St. Michael the Archangel's Mass on September 29, Martlemas or Martinmas for St. Martin of Tours on November 11, Candlemas or the Mass of Candles on February 2, and so forth. The Dutch *Kerstmis*—or *Kerst* for short—is based on the same idea.

LESSONS AND CAROLS

Before 1918, King's College Chapel in Cambridge, England, had always celebrated Christmas Eve the same way: with the Anglican service of Evensong followed by carols. That changed when thirty-four-year-old Eric Milner-White was appointed dean. Milner-White, who had been an army chaplain in World War I, felt that the Church of England needed more imaginative worship. He took a service consisting of nine carols and nine short lessons (Biblical readings) that had been created by E. W. Benson in 1880 and adapted it, adding an opening Bidding Prayer. Since 1928 the service has been broadcast on the radio every year except 1930; it even aired during World War II, when the chapel's stained glass was removed and you could hear the tarpaper flapping in the background. Today the Festival of Nine Lessons and Carols can be heard over the radio practically anywhere in the world; one grateful correspondent listened to it in a tent on the foothills of Mount Everest. Milner-White's service has been copied by churches all over the world.

Besides excellent performances by the chapel's choir, perhaps the key to the success of the Festival of Nine Lessons and Carols is the ingenious way it mixes Biblical readings and carols that reflect the content and mood of those readings, all in a way that progresses from the Fall of Adam to the Birth of Christ. The main theme of the service, according to Milner-White, "is the development of the loving purposes of God." For many, hearing the Festival of Nine Lessons and Carols over the airwaves marks the beginning of Christmas.

GIFTS

We devoted Chapters Four, Five, and Six to Christmas-time's magical or miraculous gift-givers and the various days on which they appear. Here is a summary of who to expect, when, and where:

December 5, St. Nicholas's Eve: St. Nicholas and various sidekicks or replacements in the Netherlands.

December 12, St. Lucy's Eve: St. Lucy, for girls in Tyrol, Austria.

December 24, Christmas Eve: Santa Claus in America; the Christ Child and the Weinachtsman in different parts of Germany other German-language regions; Father Christmas in England; Père Noël in France; Tante Arie in Franche-Comté, France, and Jura, Switzerland; the Christmas Gnome and Yule Goat in the Nordic countries; the Yule Lads in Iceland.

December 26, Boxing Day: gifts to the poor or one's servants in England.

December 31, New Year's Eve: St. Basil in Greece.

January 1, New Year's Day: Grandfather Frost in Russia and the former Soviet bloc; adults exchange gifts in France.

January 5, Epiphany Eve or Twelfth Night: the Magi in Spanish-speaking countries; Befana in Italy; Baboushka and Kolyáda in Russia; Berchta in some parts of Germany.

While modern Americans usually concentrate all of their gift-giving on Christmas Day, in some other places the gifts are stretched out during the days leading up to

Christmas (Iceland) or during the Twelve Day of Christmas, or they are distributed on both Christmas and Epiphany (French Canada).

KINDNESS TO ANIMALS

It was the great patron of furry friends, St. Francis of Assisi (d. 1226), who began a tradition of being especially kind to animals during the Christmas season, so that they could share in the joy of the feast. Francis encouraged farmers to give their oxen and asses extra fodder on Christmas Eve "for reverence of the Son of God, whom on such a night the Blessed Virgin Mary did lay down in the stall between the ox and the ass." Francis's reasoning was that all creation should rejoice at the birth of its Creator, and the only way dumb creatures can rejoice is with more comfort and better food. "If I could see the Emperor," he said, "I would implore him to issue a general decree that all people who are able to do so, shall throw grain and corn upon the streets, so that on this great feast day the birds might have enough to eat, especially our sisters, the larks."[4]

The saint never got the imperial backing he hoped for, but it is still the custom in many places to put out sheaves of grain for the birds on Christmas Eve and to have one's livestock abstain from labor during the Twelve Days of Christmas. Scandinavians erect an outdoor "Christmas tree" for birds made out of grain or set out a pole with a sheaf of grain. Farmers in Silesia once believed that if you had grain in your pocket during the Christmas service and gave it to your poultry afterwards, they would lay more eggs. In Hungary, wild birds are given the honor of having the last sheaf of the harvest on New Year's morning. In several European countries, horses were honored on St. Stephen's Day (December 26)—but not in Lithuania, where horses were not given extra fodder on the legendary grounds that the horse in the stable at Bethlehem refused to warm the Infant Jesus.

Besides extra food and time off work, animals were "wassailed" and "sained" (as we saw in Chapter Seven). In parts of England, cattle were formally greeted and anointed with cider. In the West Country, the ceremony took place on Twelfth Night: the family went to the stalls, drank from the wassail bowl, and put a decorated cake on the ox's horns. If the animal stayed still, good luck would come. In a similar ritual in Hereford, the oldest person of the assembly chanted:

> Here's to thy pretty face, and to thy white
>   horn,
> God send thy master a good crop of corn,
> Both wheat, rye and barley, of grains of
>   all sort,
> And next year if we live we'll drink to thee
>   again.[5]

In Hertfordshire and Sussex, bees were wassailed. In Poland, cattle were given an *opłatek* (Christmas wafer) from the Christmas Eve dinner (see Chapter Ten) and blessed with the sign of the cross. In some places cattle were sprinkled with holy water and blessed salt on St. Thomas's Eve (December 20), as the farmer said, "St. Thomas preserve thee from all sickness."[6]

It is a good thing that people are kind to animals at Christmas, for it is on this Holy Night that they possess special powers. According to folklore, deer in the forest and cattle in their stalls bend their knees at midnight on Christmas to adore the newborn King, while bees hum "a beautiful symphony of praise to the Divine Child" (although only the pious can hear it).[7] Birds sing in the night. In fact roosters crow continuously, according to *Hamlet*:

> Some say that ever 'gainst that season comes
> Wherein our Saviour's birth is celebrated,
> This bird of dawning singeth all night long.

What is more, dumb creatures gain the gift of gab, and in Latin no less. According to a medieval French play, the cock announces *Christus natus est*! ("Christ is born"), to which the ox inquires *Ubi?* ("Where?"). *Bethlehem*, brays the lamb in response, while the ass brays *Eamus!* ("Let's go!"). But be careful of eavesdropping on them. In Central Europe it is said that stabled animals gossip about anyone who listens in on their conversation on Christmas Eve.

LEISURE

Animals aren't the only ones who should take it easy during Christmastime. According to an ancient (and practical) tradition, by Christmas Eve the house is to be thoroughly cleaned, all tasks finished or removed from sight, all borrowed items returned, and no task allowed to be begun that cannot be finished by nightfall. Some places try to wrap things up even earlier. As we saw in Chapter One, all Yuletide preparations in Norway—such as chopping firewood, baking, and slaughtering—had to be completed by St. Thomas's Day, on December 21. The Apostle even took on the nickname "St. Thomas the Brewer" because all holiday beer had to be brewed by his feast day, and no more brewing could be done until after Epiphany.

During the Twelve Days of Christmas, courts and places of business would be closed, prisoners pardoned, and as little work done as possible. It was a unique period of leisure and merriment.

LIGHTS

Lights are an obvious symbol of hope during the dark days of winter, which is why the use of ceremonial lights during this time of year was common in pre-Christian days. It is no surprise that many of these customs would be embraced by Christians, who celebrate the birth of the Light of the World on Christmas Day.

One of the most symbolically rich customs of Christmas Eve is the Christmas candle, a large white candle representing Christ. In Ireland, a Christmas candle, bedecked with holly, would burn through the night and be relit on each of the twelve nights of Christmas. The entire family would pray before the candle for their living and departed loved ones. In England and Ireland, the Christmas candle often consisted of three individual candles molded together in honor of the Trinity, while in Germany a highly decorated pyramid of smaller candles called a *Weihnachtspyramide* was used, as we saw in Chapter Eight.

Another Irish custom during Christmastide was putting lights in the window. This practice originated during the times of persecution, when Mass had to be held in secret. Faithful Irish believers would place a candle in the window on Christmas Eve as a sign to any priest who happened by that this home was a safe haven in which Mass could be offered. When interrogated by the British about the meaning of this practice, the Irish replied that the lights were an invitation for Joseph and Mary to stay the night. Unthreatened by this supposed superstition, the British left them alone.

Perhaps surprisingly, candles in the window may not be the origin of one of the most familiar signs of the Christmas season: strings of light bulbs on the outside of buildings. Thanks to the invention of electricity, lights probably migrated from Christmas trees inside the home to Christmas trees in the public square (beginning in the early twentieth century) to Christmas lights on the exterior trim of houses, stores, and so forth (which gained worldwide popularity by the mid twentieth century). The lights can be large or small, white or colored, and are usually put up at the beginning of Advent and taken down on Twelfth Night (January 5) or Candlemas (February 2). Leaving up Christmas lights throughout the year is considered bad luck and a surefire way to irritate your neighbors.

An older custom comes from the peaks of the Alps, when mountain folk lit fires and then carried lanterns down, swinging them to and fro, on their way into the valley for Midnight Mass. It looked like hundreds of glow worms converging on the parish church.

MASSES

As we mentioned above, "Christmas" means "Christ's Mass." But perhaps it should be called "Christmasses." In the traditional Roman rite, three Masses are celebrated on Christmas in honor of the various aspects of the mystery of the Incarnation.

The First Mass, celebrating the Birth of Jesus to Mary in the stable in Bethlehem, is usually celebrated at midnight, the hour it is believed that the Lord was born. The Gospels do not disclose the hour of Christ's birth, but early Christians considered Wisdom 18:14–15 to be applicable:

> For while all things were in quiet silence,
> and the night was in the midst of her course,
> Thy almighty Word leapt down from heaven
> from Thy royal throne.

The Gospel read at the First Mass is the beloved passage from St. Luke's Gospel (familiar even to the un-churched from Linus in "A Charlie Brown Christmas"), from Caesar Augustus decreeing that all the world should be taxed up through the angels' Gloria. Thus the "Angels' Mass," often known as Midnight Mass, is a cherished tradition among many Catholics, even though the Roman rite does not require the First Mass to begin at that time (in Spain the First Mass begins at 3:00 a.m., where it is called *Misa de Gallo*, Mass of the Cock's Crow). Solemn Vespers or hymns and carols are often sung before Midnight Mass, during which time the church bells are rung. We have already discussed the charming custom of pealing for the Devil's funeral (see Chapter Seven).

The Second Mass, which is celebrated at dawn, is often called the "Shepherds' Mass," because of its Gospel reading, which tells how the shepherds went to the stable and worshipped the Baby Jesus—the first people outside the Holy Family to see and know the Incarnate Lord.

Finally, the Third Mass, known as the "Mass of the Divine Word," is celebrated during Christmas Day. It commemorates the *eternal* generation of the Son from the Father and our *spiritual* birth as sons of God:

> In the beginning was the Word, and the Word was with God, and the Word was God.... He came unto His own, and His own received Him not. But as many as received Him, He gave them power to be made the sons of God, to them that believe in His name. Who are born, not of blood, nor of the will of the flesh, nor of the will of man, but of God.

As their names suggest, each of the three Masses focuses primarily on one aspect of the Incarnation, but not exclusively. The interplay of themes allows the participant to contemplate the entire mystery no matter what Mass he attends.

Although it was not required, it was a custom for many of the faithful in the Middle Ages to attend all three Masses. Today, the Midnight Mass is the most popular. In Bethlehem, the Church of St. Catherine, owned by the Catholic Church, is adjacent to the Basilica of the Nativity, maintained by the Greek Orthodox Patriarchate of Jerusalem. After the (Catholic) Latin Patriarch of Jerusalem celebrates Midnight Mass in the Church of St. Catherine, a statue of the Infant Jesus is placed on the altar and then processed under the Basilica of the

Nativity to the Grotto of the Nativity, the cave where it is believed that Jesus was born. The statue is placed on a silver star that marks the exact spot of Christ's Nativity. The infancy narrative according to St. Luke is then sung; at the words, "she laid him in a manger," the statue is lifted up and placed in a crib hewn out of rock not far from the star. Other churches, both Catholic and Protestant, also place a statue of the Infant Jesus in their Nativity sets at their Christmas service.

PAGEANTS

Like other high points of the Church calendar, Christmas was the occasion of devout plays, dramatic performances that explained the meaning of the mystery being commemorated. We saw in Chapter Eight how one Christmas pageant about Adam and Eve led to the creation of the Christmas tree, and in Chapter Two how St. Francis of Assisi's *tableau vivant* of the Nativity led to the creation of Nativity sets. By the late Middle Ages these plays had become elaborate pageants, public entertainment (usually held outside the church on a movable stage) that consisted of various scenes from history and legend.

Alas, even pious plays can enter a late-Elvis Vegas stage, and by the fifteenth century the so-called miracle play had grown decadent and irreverent. Church officials either forbade them or exiled them from the church sanctuary. The Protestant Reformers were not fond of these performances either and likewise prohibited them.

Nativity plays did, however, survive in some parts of Europe and eventually made their way to the United States, thanks mostly to German immigrants. Here is an account of the alleged first Christmas pageant held in Boston in 1851:

> [T]he children of the parish, dressed as Oriental shepherds, carrying bundles of food, linen, and other gifts, marched in solemn procession to the crib in front of the altar, singing Christmas carols. They honored the Divine Child by offering their presents, reciting prayers, and chanting hymns. The parish priest accepted the offerings, which were afterward distributed to the poor. The children in their Oriental costumes, their hands folded devoutly, left the church in a street procession after the service. This performance attracted such attention and admiration that it had to be repeated twice during Christmas week upon the urgent request of both Catholics and Protestants from all over the city who were anxious to witness the "new" pageant.[8]

It was performances such as these that led to our modern school Christmas plays and Christmas pageants.

SEASON'S GREETINGS

Most languages have a fairly straightforward way of formulating their Christmas greetings: take the name of the feast and add a word like "happy," "joyful," or "good." Hence the German *Froehliche Weihnachten*, the Spanish *Feliz Navidad*, the Portuguese *Feliz Natal*, the Italian *Buon Natale*, the French *Joyeux Noël*, the Icelandic *Gledileg Jol*, the Danish *Glædelig Jul*, the Finnish *Hyvaa joulua*, and the Norwegian and Swedish *God Jul*.

Once again English had to be a little different. The first recorded instance of "Merry Christmas" did not have the desired effect. John Fisher was a Catholic bishop imprisoned in the Tower of London for refusing to acknowledge King Henry VIII as Supreme Head of the Church of England. On December 22, 1534, the impoverished prisoner wrote to Henry's chief minister Thomas Cromwell and asked for a shirt and a sheet, some spiritual books, and a priest to hear his confession. Fisher concluded his letter with: "And this our Lord God send you a merry Christmas, and a comfortable, to your heart's desire."[9] We don't know whether Fisher ever got the Christmas presents he requested, but he was executed six months later to the day and eventually canonized a saint in the Catholic Church. Five years after Fisher's death, Cromwell would be imprisoned in the same tower and executed, unwept, unhonored, and unsung.

What did Fisher and his contemporaries mean by "merry"? According to one theory, in the sixteenth century "merry" was synonymous with "blessed, peaceful, pleasant" and therefore expressed "spiritual joys rather than earthly happiness."[10] The original meaning of "Merry England" was that England is graced, not that she is cheerful. As we have seen, the original punctuation of the Christmas carol "God Rest Ye Merry Gentlemen" is not "God rest ye, merry gentlemen" but "God rest ye merry, gentlemen." In other words, the song is not greeting chipper gentlemen; it is invoking Christian peace, as in "God keep you in peace, gentlemen." Today, "merry Christmas" is often replaced with "Happy holidays" or "Season's greetings" for fear of giving offense, but most folks have no idea how "offensive" the old phrase really is. It is not just that Christ or His Mass or His birth are being recalled but that the greeter is essentially calling down a blessing from Heaven.

But although "Merry Christmas" has a high, almost sacred meaning behind it, it has also come to take on a more vulgar connotation. Merriment can signify public festivity, and public festivity often involves public tipsiness. Charles Dickens uses "Merry Christmas" in his writings more than any other holiday greeting, but the Victorian upper and middle classes nevertheless associated merriment with lowbrow revelry and antics. In 1932, King George V used the phrase "Happy Christmas" in the first

A Christmas toast. *E. A. Abbey*

royal Christmas message, and Queen Elizabeth II has done the same ever since. "[*H*]*appy* overtook *merry* in Britain during the 1930s"—with America holding on to the original English greeting and England moving on to the ostensibly more respectable innovation—"[p]erhaps as a result of the royal preference," conjectures one author.[11]

Eastern Orthodox and Eastern-Rite Catholics have a beautiful Christmas greeting. "Christ is born!" says one person. "Glorify Him!" replies the other.

WASSAILING

We have already mentioned two meanings of wassailing, first as a toast and then as a drink (see Chapter Ten). A third meaning is to greet someone, often with a wassail bowl and often door to door, on Christmas Day. In seventeenth-century England, "wassail wenches" went around town with a wassail bowl singing and offering a swig from the bowl in return for a donation:

> Good Dame, here at your door
> Our Wassail we begin
> We are all maidens poor,

We pray now let us in,
With our Wassail.[12]

Another kind of wassailing you do not hear much about these days is as a form of "saining," that is, as we saw in Chapter Seven, blessing something. In the old days, folks would wassail livestock as a way of invoking good health upon them, but it was once more common to wassail fruit trees, usually on Epiphany Eve. As the seventeenth-century poet Robert Herrick wrote:

Wassail the trees, that they may bear
You many a plum, and many a pear:
For more or less fruits they will bring,
As you do give them wassailing.

Strategies ranged from flattery to threats. In some parts of the England, folks formed a circle around a tree and chanted:

Here's to thee, old apple tree
Whence thou mayst bud and when thou
    mayst blow
And whence thou mayst bear apples enow:
Hats full, caps full,
Bushels, bushels, sacks full,
And my pockets full too!
Huzza! Huzza!

But in other places, they warned:

> Apple tree, apple tree
> Bear good fruit,
> Or down with your top
> And up with your root!

Our favorite example of wassailing combines both approaches. In old Romania, the husband and wife played good cop–bad cop. At Christmas, the husband roamed through the orchard with an axe, approaching barren trees and threatening to cut them down. Each time the wife would intervene and say, "Oh no, I am sure that this tree will be as heavy with fruit next spring as my fingers are with dough this day."[13]

THE YULE LOG

The Yule log or Christmas log is commonly believed to be a holdover from pagan German customs, but the problem with this theory is that there is no record of a Yule log until the sixteenth century, long after Germany's conversion to Christianity. What we do know is this: the custom of the Yule log probably began in Germany, and from there it spread to most European nations, the United States, Canada, and beyond.

The idea is simple. A large log is burned in the home during the Christmas season (in some places, from

Christmas Eve to Candlemas Day on February 2). How large a log? Sometimes, it was an entire tree trunk. There is a story from the nineteenth century that when a visitor asked the owner of an English cottage why the flagstones leading up to his front door were all broken, the man explained that a draft horse stepped on them as it was dragging home the Christmas log. Apparently, open hearth fireplaces were quite commodious.

Prior to modern heating, the Yule log had special significance as a source of warmth and a symbol of light. And in the antebellum South, it even functioned as a beacon of (temporary) freedom. Slaves did not have to work as long as the Yule log burned, and so they often doused it with water to delay its consumption. Hence the old Southern proverb about wet wood having "as much water as a Christmas log."[14]

The ideal wood depends on local tradition. The English prefer ash, pine, or oak; the French insist on wood from a fruit tree; the Scottish look for birch, and the Serbs oak. In the United States, the only "rule" is that it is bad luck to buy one's Christmas log and good luck to find it on one's own property. Here in Texas, I recommend that we appoint mountain cedar (Ashe juniper) for the job: it may be a bit small, but there are too many of them, and since German settlers used to make charcoal out of them, they are no strangers to being used as fuel. But if you can't have a fire because you live in a tiny apartment in New York City, you can watch on TV or livestream the famous WPIX Yule Log, which has been broadcast every year since 1966.

When the Yule log is chosen also varies according to place. In England, it is selected on Candlemas (February 2) and set aside to dry for almost a year. Elsewhere, the log is chosen on Christmas Eve day. In France the entire family goes out to find it, while in Norway the father alone would conduct the search. When a suitable log was found, it was often decorated with ribbons before being dragged home in a joyful family procession. Passersby would raise their hats at the procession, and if the log was being dragged through the snow, the youngest member of the family got to ride on top of it.

In Palmer Lake, Colorado, townspeople participate in an annual Yule Log scavenger hunt sometime in mid-December. A tree is cut down and its trunk hidden. The person who finds it gets to ride on it as it is ceremoniously marched into Town Hall and burned. In Steamboat Springs, Colorado, the scavengers must answer riddles about local history to find the log; the winner receives a prize of one hundred dollars.

When the log is placed on the hearth and lit, it is done with great ceremony. In Dalmatia, Montenegro, Lombardy, France, and elsewhere, the log was splashed with wine and blessed by the father in the name of the Holy Trinity. In most places, it was lit by a remnant from last year's Yule log, as Robert Herrick attests in a 1695 poem:

With the last year's brand
Light the new block, and
For good success in his spending,
On your Psalteries play,
That sweet luck may
Come while the log is a-teending.[15]

Herrick also mentions that the maids who help with the lighting must have clean hands or they will kill the fire. In the Scottish Highlands, the father would find a twisted root or stump on December 24 and carve it into the shape of an old woman. The "Christmas Old Wife," who represented evil and misfortune, was then thrown onto the evening fire to ensure good luck for the upcoming year. In Newfoundland, after the "Back-Junk" or Yule log was lit, the father would fire a gun from the porch to let his neighbors know that the deed was done.

When the log is almost gone, a portion is saved in order to start the log next Christmas. Remnants can also be put in the fire again for protection during storms, and they are useful in curing sick cattle, preventing mildew, and keeping toothaches and chilblains at bay. Similarly, the ashes of a Yule log help cows calve, produce good crops, and make well water sweet.

Chapter Twelve

THE TOPSY-TURVY TWELVE DAYS OF CHRISTMAS: IT'S NOT JUST A LONG CAROL

For most of Christian history, the Twelve Days of Christmas—the period between the two great feasts of Christmas on December 25 and the Epiphany on January 6—was the real time to celebrate. Courts and businesses would be closed during this time, the firewood would already be chopped and the food already processed, and everyone would abstain from work as much as he could. Feasting and gift-giving did not end on Christmas Day but continued (on and off) for the next week and a half. As we saw in the last chapter, even the farm animals got some extra food and a break from labor, in honor of the ox and the ass reputedly present at the Lord's birth.

Theatrical reenactments of the Christmas story were often held during the Twelve Days, along with other pageants and masquerades. In the home, the Christmas tree stayed up until the day after Epiphany and was lit every night. Families would gather around it to pray and sing Christmas carols.

But perhaps the most distinguishing characteristic of the Twelve Days of Christmas was its topsy-turvy elements, customs that inverted almost every social ranking of the day. Rich and poor, laity and clergy, young and old, servant and master, enlisted and officer, man and woman—everything and everyone would be turned upside down. Inversion practices are not unique to Christendom: the ancient Mesopotamians had a primitive version, and the Romans celebrated the Saturnalia from December 17 to as late as December 23 with masquerading, loud clothes, and masters either serving their slaves dinner or dining with them (slaves were even allowed to wear the *pileus*, the felt cap signifying emancipation).

But customs that upend things take on new meaning in light of Christian belief. In Acts 17:6, St. Luke records that Jews at Thessalonica were envious of the Christians as "these who have turned the world upside down." Christianity does indeed turn the world upside down, for it rejoices in the Creator's becoming a creature, nestling in the womb of one of His creations and being born a helpless babe. As His Mother declared in her Magnificat,

> He hath put down the mighty from their seat, and hath exalted the humble. He hath filled the hungry with good things; and the rich he hath sent empty away.

Topsy-turvy customs are a giddy imitation of the ultimate inversion, that God became man and that the King of Kings came as a servant.

ST. STEPHEN'S DAY (DECEMBER 26)

St. Stephen, one of the first seven men ordained a deacon by the guidance of the Holy Spirit, is called the "Proto-Martyr," for in being stoned to death by order of the Sanhedrin, he became the first disciple to voluntarily shed his blood for the Faith.[1] Stephen is a model of that divinely-infused love known in the Christian tradition as *agape* or *caritas* or "charity," because as a deacon he served the poor and as a martyr he forgave his murders.

BOXING DAY

St. Stephen's Day is also known as Boxing Day—after a custom that imitates the saint's charity. The name may be derived from opening the poor boxes in the church and distributing their contents to the poor; or it may come from the custom of giving servants Christmas boxes for

"I'll raise your salary!" *Sol Eytinge Jr.*

their journey home on their day off. Either way, the idea is that the rich give to the poor and masters to their servants. In the British and Canadian militaries, this principle has been applied to officers and enlisted personnel. In Canada, officers serve Christmas dinner to non-commissioned officers, and NCOs serve stewards. Throughout the Christmas season, "rules are bent in a playful way. Commanding officers frequently switch roles and tunics with the youngest member of the unit. This soldier then becomes the honorary commander for the day. The remainder of the officers and the warrant officers and sergeants exchange their jackets and tunics for chef's hats and aprons."[2] And on Christmas morning in the British army, officers on deployment go to the beds of their enlisted men and serve them a "Gunfire"—hot tea mixed with a shot of rum.

In many places Boxing Day remains the customary occasion for giving gifts to one's servants, paperboy, postal worker, and so on.

HORSES

Not all customs associated with December 26 point so lucidly to the life of St. Stephen. The holy deacon is considered the patron saint of horses despite the fact that he has no scriptural connection to them. Some speculate that this patronage may have something to do with the relief from work that domestic animals, at the behest of St. Francis of Assisi, enjoyed during the Twelve Days of Christmas, but no one is certain.

In any case, the association stuck, especially in rural areas. Horse parades, horse races, and a "St. Stephen's ride" in a sleigh or wagon were common, as was decorating one's horse and riding it to the church for a blessing. Horse food (hay or oats) would also be blessed on this day. But this is not to say that horses enjoyed every aspect of the feast. In some parts of sixteenth-century England, people let out their horses' blood with a knife "because St. Stephen was killed with stones."[3] Happily, the equestrian motif survives in less violent ways today. In several nations it is customary to bake special breads in the form of horseshoes to honor St. Stephen.[4]

RITUAL SCOURGING

Speaking of violence, there was a pre-Christian winter practice of one group's ritually scourging another as an act not of cruelty or punishment but of kindness: the scourging either drove away bad spirits or imparted the sacred qualities of the tree whose branches were being used. One proof that the act was beneficent is that the person who was whipped was supposed to give his whipper a treat afterwards!

Christians adapted these practices to their own holy season. In Orlagau, Germany, on St. Stephen's Day, girls would beat their parents and godparents with green fir-branches, and menservants would beat their masters with rosemary sticks, saying:

> Fresh green! Long life!
> Give me a bright ___ [pick your treat]

In the same region, the boys got their turn on St. John's Day. But in the Saxon *Erzgebirge*, it was the opposite: young men whipped women and girls on St. Stephen's Day with birch-rods, preferably when they were still in bed, and on St. John's Day the women paid the men back.

Childermas or Innocents' Day (see below) was an especially popular occasion for these customs. In parts of Germany, children would beat passers-by with birch-boughs and be rewarded with apples, nuts, and other treats on the feast of the Holy Innocents. But usually it was the children who got the short end of the stick, awakening on Childermas morning to a whipping from their parents in imitation of Herod's cruelty to the innocent babes of Bethlehem.

ST. JOHN'S DAY (DECEMBER 27)

Like St. Stephen, St. John the Apostle and Evangelist is associated with charity; his writings tenderly emphasize the love of God[5]—and because John was blessed by Christ's special love for him. Although Our Lord made St. Peter the head of His Church, He retained a personal affection for the "beloved disciple." This fondness is all the more endearing given the fact that Our Lord also referred to John and his older brother St. James the Great as "sons of thunder," most likely for their fiery tempers.[6]

IN VINO CARITAS

It has been said that St. John was the only Apostle who did not die a martyr because he had already testified to the Cross by standing at its foot with Mary, the Mother of God. This does not mean that no attempts on his life were ever made. The saint's most famous brush with death (as far as popular folklore is concerned) is when his enemies tried to kill him by poisoning his cup of wine. Some say that when the Divine John (as he is called in the East) made the sign of the cross over the cup, it split in half, thus spilling the poison. Others claim that his blessing neutralized the deadly beverage and allowed him to enjoy it unharmed.

Either way, this pious story is the inspiration for a charming custom that almost literally toasts the memory of the saint. The Catholic Church has a blessing of wine or cider specifically for this feast:

> O Lord God, deign to bless and consecrate
> with Thy right hand this cup of wine and

of any drink whatsoever: and grant that by the merits of St. John the Apostle and Evangelist all who believe in Thee and who drink from this cup may be blessed and protected. And as Blessed John drank poison from the cup and remained completely unharmed, may all who drink from this cup on this day in honor of Blessed John be, by his merits, rescued from every sickness of poison and from every kind of harm; and, offering themselves up body and soul, may they be delivered from all fault. Through Christ our Lord. Amen.

Bless, O Lord, this drink, Thy creation: that it may be a salutary remedy for all who consume it: and grant through the invocation of Thy holy name that whoever tastes of it may, by Thy generosity, receive health of the soul as well as of the body. Through Christ our Lord. Amen.

And may the blessing of almighty God, Father, Son, and Holy Ghost, descend upon this wine, Thy creation, and upon any drink whatsoever, and remain forever. Amen.[7]

It was once customary in Austria to bring one's beverage to church on this day so that the priest could give this blessing after Mass. Later that night, the wine was poured into everyone's glass before dinner. The father then took his glass, touched it to the mother's and said, "I drink to you the love of St. John," to which the mother replied, "I thank you for the love of St. John." Both took a sip before the mother turned to the oldest child and repeated the ritual, the oldest child turned to the next oldest, and so forth. The last one to receive St. John's love gave it back to the father, thus closing the family circle.[8] The wine could be mulled to combat the winter cold.

And it need not all be consumed in one day. St. John's wine was used throughout the year as a cure for illnesses and at weddings, as a protection against lightning (!), and as a preservative for one's other wine (it was believed that adding a dash of St. John's wine to your other casks would keep them safe from harm).

THE HOLY INNOCENTS (DECEMBER 28)

In an attempt to kill Jesus, Whom he thought was a rival for his crown, King Herod ordered the slaughter of all boys in Bethlehem two years old and under (Matthew 2:16–18). St. Matthew's Gospel does not tell us how many died in the massacre. The Byzantine liturgy mentions 14,000, the Syrian churches say 64,000, and some medieval authors, inspired by Revelation 14:3, speak of a staggering 144,000. But based on fertility rates and the size of the population of Bethlehem and its environs at the time, a more realistic estimate puts the number of the slain somewhere between 10 and 20.

Matthew's account is also silent about the date of the massacre, except for hinting that it happened within two years of the apparition of the Christmas star that guided the Magi. The Western churches, from what we can tell, have always kept the feast of "Childermas" (Children's Mass) on December 28, ever since it first began being celebrated in the fifth century. Thus the Roman calendar presents an interesting array of Christ's friends on December 26, 27, and 28: first St. Stephen, the Proto-Martyr who is a martyr by will, love, and blood; then St. John the Evangelist, who is a martyr by will and love (John is considered a martyr because of the attempts made on his life even though he died a natural death); and lastly, the Holy Innocents, who are martyrs by blood alone. As St. Augustine says of them, "They are the first buds of the Church killed by the frost of persecution."[9]

THE HUMBLE SHALL BE EXALTED

Understandably, Innocents' Day is a magnet for topsy-turvy customs that involve young and old. In many religious communities, the novices had the privilege of sitting at the head of the table at meals and meetings, and the last person who had taken vows in the monastery or convent got to be superior for a day. Young monks and nuns would receive congratulations and have "baby food," such as hot cereal, served to them for dinner.[10]

A similar flip-flop occurred in the family. Customs such as decorating the crib or blessing the baby were standard ways of observing the feast, and the youngest child was allowed special privileges and honors, even becoming master of the household.

Not all customs, however, boded well for the young 'uns. As we saw in the "Ritual Scourging" section above, some children awoke to a spanking from their parents— "to remind them of the sufferings of the Innocents!"[11] In Central Europe, groups of children would revive a pre-Christian fertility rite by going up to women and girls with branches and twigs and chanting:

> Many years of healthy life,
> Happy girl, happy wife:
> Many children, hale and strong,
> Nothing harmful, nothing wrong,
> Much to drink and more to eat;
> Now we beg a kindly treat.

They would then swat them gently with branches and twigs.[12]

In the Philippines and Spanish-speaking countries, Childermas is the equivalent of April's Fools Day, a time of pranks and practical jokes, called *inocentadas*.

Lastly, Childermas was an important day for the Boy Bishop (see Chapter Four).

SUPERSTITIONS

All of Christendom once abstained from servile work during the Twelve Days of Christmas, but there was an extra incentive to do so on the Feast of the Holy Innocents. According to an old superstition, it is bad luck to begin any new work on this day, either because it will never be finished or because it will come to a bad end. Either way, the superstition was strong enough to keep leaders like King Louis XI of France and King Edward IV of England from doing any business on December 28. Perhaps the rationale is that just as the Holy Innocents' lives were cut tragically short, so too would be any work begun on their feast day.[13]

In German-speaking countries, Christianity almost literally baptized the pagan fear of souls wandering the earth after the winter solstice. According to legend, the souls of unbaptized children are chaperoned by the frightening Hel, the Germanic goddess of the underworld (from whose name the English word "Hell" is derived). Each child carries a pitcher filled with the tears he or she shed that year. But thanks to the mercy of God, if on Innocents' Day a person hears a cry in the howling wind or sees a ghostly shape fluttering in the dark, he should call out a Christian name. The "baptismal" name frees the child from Lady Hel's grip and allows him to join the Holy Innocents in eternal bliss.[14]

NEW YEAR'S EVE (DECEMBER 31)

New Year's Eve has been an occasion for merrymaking (and worse) ever since the Roman festival of the *Kalendae Januarii*. The early Christian Church was opposed to the pagan proclivity for excess and instead kept January 1 as a day of fasting and penance. To this day, as far as the Church is concerned, the start of the civic year is a non-event.

Nevertheless, because it is only natural to mark the end of an old year and the beginning of a new one, and because it is a good idea to ask God's blessings on the future, Christians eventually adopted aspects of the Roman new year and added a few of their own.

SILVESTERABEND

St. Sylvester was pope during the reign of Constantine, the Roman emperor who ended the persecution of the Church. One legend even claims that Sylvester baptized Constantine after the latter was miraculously cured from leprosy.

There is a simple reason why the saint's feast falls on this day: after twenty-one years of service to God as pope, Sylvester died and was buried on December 31, 335. That said, there is something appropriate about preparing for the new civic year—which falls within the time when our hearts are filled with hope for "peace on earth"—by celebrating the first bishop of Rome to occupy the throne of Peter during a time of civic peace.

In many countries New Year's Eve is known as Sylvester Night (*Silvesterabend* or *Silvesternacht* in German). In France and French Canada it is traditional for the father to bless the members of his family and for the children to thank their parents for all of their love and care.[15] In Central Europe, a pre-Christian ritual of scaring away demons with loud noises was retained; from this is derived our custom of fireworks and artillery salutes in welcome of the new year. In Austria, December 31 was sometimes called *Rauchnacht* or "Incense Night," when the paterfamilias of the family went through the house and barn purifying them with incense and holy water.[16]

SUPERSTITIONS

Sylvester Night was also a favorite occasion for attempts to peer into the upcoming year. The reading of tea leaves was once popular, as was pouring spoonfuls of molten lead into water and interpreting the future from the shapes it took. Young maidens prayed to St. Sylvester in traditional rhymes, asking him for a good husband and hoping through his intercession to catch a glimpse of Mr. Right in their dreams or in a mirror.[17]

RELIGIOUS SERVICES

On the more pious side of things were vigil services of various kinds to thank God for the gifts of the year and seek blessings for the new. To this day, the Catholic Church grants a plenary indulgence, under the usual conditions, for a public recitation of the great Latin hymn of thanksgiving, the *Te Deum*, on the last day of the year.[18]

A century ago in England and Scotland, the night was marked by penitential "Watch Night" services, which could consist of testimonies from members of the congregation about God's blessings during the year or the making of good resolutions. Several denominations, especially among African Americans, have a tradition of Watch Night services. It is said that slaves gathered in their churches on the night of December 31, 1862, to wait for Abraham Lincoln's Emancipation Proclamation to take effect the next day. Ever since then, Watch Night services have been popular in black churches.

AULD LANG SYNE

The Scottish, as we have seen, celebrate New Year's Eve with zest. The (Presbyterian) Church of Scotland had suppressed Christmas in that land, and so all of the Scots' pent-up desire for celebration was redirected to the New Year. Even after Christmas celebrations made a comeback in the mid-twentieth century, the so-called "Daft Days"—New Year's Eve ("Hogmanay") and New Year's Day ("Ne'er Day")—are considered *the* Scottish national holiday and the "chief of all festivals."[19]

One Scottish custom to catch on elsewhere is the signing of *Auld Lang Syne* at the beginning of the new year. In 1788 the great poet Robert Burns took an old Scottish folk song and adapted it. Burns described his poem as "an old song, of the olden times, and which has never been in print, nor even in manuscript until I took it down from an old man."[20] Some of the lines predate Burns, but the finished product is uniquely his. The standard English version is:

> Should old acquaintance be forgot,
> And never brought to mind?
> Should old acquaintance be forgot,
> And auld lang syne?
>
> For auld lang syne, my dear,
> For auld lang syne,
> We'll take a cup of kindness yet,
> For auld lang syne.

The meaning can be cryptic to those unfamiliar with the Scots language. "Auld lang syne" is Scots for "old long since," and in the poem it functions as "for the sake of old times." The song is popular not only on New Year's Eve but also at funerals, graduations, and other farewell events.

THE COUNTDOWN

The Scottish also had a fondness for gathering before a public clock or bell tower and celebrating at the stroke of midnight. In Edinburgh all eyes were on the lighted clock-face of Auld and Faithful Tron (Church), while in London displaced Scots were attuned to the midnight chime of St. Paul's Cathedral.

The Scottish were not alone in taking advantage of modern time-keeping devices. In Spain and other Spanish-speaking areas it was considered good luck to eat twelve grapes at the twelve strokes of midnight. In Austria, *krapfen*, apricot-jam doughnuts, are traditionally eaten when the clock strikes twelve on New Year's Eve. In Greece, the father of the family steps outside at midnight and smashes a pomegranate for good luck. He then cuts the St. Basil cake or *Vasilopita*: the first piece is dedicated to Jesus Christ and the second to the Church, while additional pieces are for absent loved ones. Finally, those present each get a piece, beginning with the oldest. Even the baby must have some to ensure good luck for the new year. And the person who gets the piece with the coin in it is guaranteed good fortune.

One custom familiar to most Americans is the ball drop in New York City's Time Square. After the *New York Times* moved into the new building on One Times Square, the newspaper promoted its new headquarters with a fireworks display on December 31, 1904. The event attracted twenty thousand spectators, so the *Times* repeated the event in 1905 and 1906. For the 1907 celebration, *Times* owner Adolph Ochs decided to take advantage of the rather recently harnessed power of electricity with a hundred incandescent light bulbs adorning a ball made out of wood and iron that was lowered down the building's flagpole at 11:59 p.m. The ball drop has taken place every year since except 1942 and 1943 (war-time blackouts), even though the *Times* moved out of One Times Square in 1913. Today the ball is illuminated by a computerized LED lighting system and ceremonially lit by a special guest as the mayor of New York City stands nearby. The ball drop is accompanied by musical perfor-mances and attracts extensive TV coverage and over a million spectators each year. It has also inspired copycats across the world.

NEW YEAR'S DAY (JANUARY 1)

FEAST OF THE CIRCUMCISION

In compliance with the Old Law, Jesus was circumcised eight days after He was born. Once December 25 was fixed as the feast day celebrating Jesus' birth, January 1 became the day to commemorate His circumcision. There is a slightly dolorous note in remembering the first time that Jesus Christ shed blood for humanity (and as a baby, no less), but the note fit in well with the Christian lament over pagan revelries. Even before the Feast of the Circum-cision (as we noted above), early Christians observed January 1 as a day of fasting and penance in opposition to the revelries of their pagan counterparts.

But because the circumcision was also the occasion when Jesus was formally given His holy name and made a member of the Holy Family, it is difficult to resist an impulse to celebrate. Over time, this impulse (combined with the joy of a new year and the close of the Christmas Octave) prevailed, and Christian customs grew as festive as the pagan, perhaps more so. In 1969, the Feast of the Circumcision was replaced on the Roman Calendar by the Solemnity of Mary, the Holy Mother of God. But below are a few highlights of practices that evolved in the time of the traditional feast day.

FEAST OF FOOLS

In the eleventh century, the Catholic Church instituted special feast days for the ranks of the clergy: St. Stephen's Day (December 26) was for deacons, St. John's Day (December 27) was for priests, Holy Innocents' Day (December 28) was for choir boys, and the Circumcision (January 1) was for subdeacons. The Feast of Fools first emerged out of the subdeacons' feast day on January 1. In France, where the practice was the most popular, a Bishop of Fools was chosen by lot from among the sub-diaconate (and later the peasantry), draped in pontifical regalia, and allowed to preside over the recitation of the Divine Office. Practical jokes were played on the Fool and vice versa. The Feast of Fools soon took on different forms in different places. In England, the head fool was known as the Lord of Misrule and in Scotland as the Abbot of Unreason; he was placed in charge of the often wild revelries throughout the Twelve Days. Although the upper echelons of the Church frowned upon these excesses, some priests left money in their wills for their upkeep.

FEAST OF THE ASS

Another popular form of entertainment that usually took place on New Year's Day was the Feast of the Ass, which began as a play honoring all of the donkeys mentioned in the Bible.[21] Pride of place went to the donkey that witnessed our Savior's birth in the manger and that carried Him and His Mother into Egypt. Poems in praise of the ass, "so beautiful, so strong and trim," were sung in its honor, and asinine elements even crept into a special Mass. After a procession to the church, a donkey (possibly a wooden figure) would be placed near the altar and Mass celebrated. At the end of Mass, instead of saying *Ite missa est* ("Go, the Mass is ended"), the priest brayed thrice, and instead of saying *Deo gratias* ("Thanks be to God") the congregation responded with three heehaws. Understandably, the Church did not tolerate this practice for very long.

GIFT GIVING

January 1 was when the ancient Romans exchanged gifts—of sweet pastry, precious stones, lamps, or coins— along with good wishes for the new year. The custom, called *strenae*, has been preserved in the tradition of *étrennes* in France, where it is on New Year's Day rather than Christmas that stockings are stuffed with treats, children receive gifts, and large family dinners are held; in fact, there is traditionally more festivity on New Year's Day in France than on Christmas.

In Germany, there was a custom of giving "New Year boxes" to tradespeople. And some countries use this day as the occasion to give presents to persons who make regular deliveries to the home. Decades ago, it was the milkman, the mailman, the diaper man (remember him?), and the paper boy. Now, of course, it is the abbreviated workers of USPS, FedEx, UPS, and DHL.

NEW YEAR CALLING

Calling is the custom of formally visiting people to pay one's respects, and in France New Year calling was once a hallowed tradition. Family, friends, and even professional associates were expected to call on each other. In Brittany the new year's wish took on a religious form: "I wish you a good year and Paradise at the end of your days."[22]

Until the middle of the nineteenth century, New Year calling was also a staple of New York City. Thanks to the lingering influence of the Dutch, New Yorkers devoted the day to a "universal interchange of visits": "Every door was thrown wide open," writes one observer. "It was a breach of etiquette to omit any acquaintance in these annual calls, when old friendships were renewed and family differences amicably settled. A hearty welcome was extended even to strangers of presentable appearance." We don't understand how anyone was at home to receive a call when everyone was supposed to be out calling, but somehow the system worked—so well that it became rather raucous. "The ceremony of calling was a burlesque. There was a noisy and hilarious greeting, a glass of wine was swallowed hurriedly, everybody shook hands all round, and the callers dashed out and rushed into the carriage and were driven rapidly to the next house."[23]

Our contemporary custom of wishing someone a happy New Year is a pale shadow of this rollicking tradition.

GREETING CARDS

Another variation of New Year calling is the Christmas card, which actually began as a New Year's greeting card. In the mid-nineteenth century, more affordable postal rates made the practice feasible, and within decades the custom was well established. Around 1850, Louis Prang, a German immigrant to Boston, began the practice of exchanging hand-made holiday cards with his friends. By 1865 he was printing multi-colored cards and selling them throughout the United States. To this day he is considered the "Father of the Greeting Card Industry." In the 1950s the American family sent out an average of fifty Christmas cards every year, a total of two billion. Today, emails and social media have put a dent in the greeting card industry.

SUPERSTITIONS

New Year calling also intersected with a superstition called "first-footing," the belief that certain characteristics of the first person to pass through the door on New Year's Day would affect the welfare of the family for the rest of the year. It was bad luck for a woman to first-foot, and so great measures were taken to have a boy or man be the first in the door on the first day of the year. In some parts of England, young urchins would go from house to house in the pre-dawn hours singing songs, and one of them would be admitted into the kitchen to provide good luck for all the year; in other places, a specially designated boy or bachelor called the "lucky bird" served as the local first-footer. In London, some restaurateurs made sure that a man opened the restaurant on New Year's morning rather than the waitresses. But women were not only the ones who bore the brunt of this prejudice: the first-footer also had to be dark-haired (blond and red-haired males brought bad luck), and he should never be flat-footed but have an instep that water could pass under!

A similar but happily non-misogynistic superstition is the belief that everything you do on New Year's Day determines the rest of the year. Based on the principle that "a good beginning makes a good ending," this superstition led folks to wear new clothes on January 1, to stuff their pockets with money, and to eat plentifully.[24] Similarly, you would not want to sleep through your

alarm clock on New Year's morning or be late for anything on that day because you would then be stuck in that
pattern for the entire year. (Greek entertainment on New
Year's Eve is based on a similar logic: folks at home
mostly play card games with the hope that if they are
lucky tonight, they will be lucky all next year.)

TWELFTH NIGHT (JANUARY 5)

Inversion customs can take place any time during the
Twelve Days of Christmas, and sometimes even after (for
example, Mardi Gras in New Orleans). But a number of
them migrated to the final night. On the evening of January 5, a King Cake would be baked with a bean or coin
in it; whoever discovered the object in his cake would be
King for the occasion. In England, an entire court would
be chosen by drawing the name of a character from a hat
and assuming that role for the rest of the night. There was
also an element of charity to these celebrations: in France
a large piece of cake was set aside for a poor person and
a collection taken for the education of a promising disadvantaged youngster.[25]

But perhaps the most memorable aspect of Twelfth
Night was cross-dressing. Christmastime cross-dressing is a kind of "mumming," the act of disguising one-
self as part of a festivity, usually tied to some kind of
pageantry or stage performance. The pageantry could
be grand and formal, as when English noblemen under
the direction of a "Master of Revels" impersonated

emperors, popes, and cardinals for the amusement of Richard II in 1377. Or it could be raucous and informal, as when common folk smeared their faces with soot or paint, wore brightly colored costumes or the garments of the opposite sex, and went from door to door trick-or-treat–style, asking for goodies from their neighbors and making mild mischief. Christmastime cross-dressing like this is still popular in places such as Newfoundland and Labrador.

Scrooge declines to donate for the relief of the poor at Christmas. *Sol Eytinge Jr.*

As for theatrical performances, the nobles enjoyed a good "masque," a courtly drama involving elaborate costumes, dancing, music, and audience participation, while the lowbrow enjoyed what eventually became known in England as "pantomime," a silly play involving a matronly character played by a generally unattractive man in drag, plenty of earthy humor, and audience participation.

In any event, the association of cross-dressing with the evening of January 5 was strong enough to allow William Shakespeare to call his play involving a female character disguised as a man "Twelfth Night." At least, that is one theory about the origin of the title.[26]

CONCLUDING REFLECTIONS

Although the topsy-turvy customs of Christmastime have not all become extinct, they have fallen on hard times. Catholic Church officials consistently tried to stem abuses throughout the Middle Ages, and the Reformers (especially the Puritans) were only too eager to deliver the coup de grâce. Henry VIII forbade children to be "stranglie decked" as "priestes, bishoppes, and women." His daughter Queen Mary restored the practice, but it was made illegal again by her successor Elizabeth. Factors contributing to the decline of the Twelve Days in the United States include the rise of Santa Claus and "Dickensian" Christmas customs, secular New Year's Eve parties, and the Christmas marketing season. Finally, the twelve-day unit of time was ruptured when the Catholic Church in the United States and in other countries moved the Feast of the Epiphany from January 6 to a nearby Sunday.

'Tis a shame. Think of the kind of movie where two people temporarily exchange bodies and are forced to live each other's lives—the classic "body-swap" or "body-switch" plot. In these stories the characters usually gain a deeper appreciation of each other's daily trials and tribulations, as well as a greater insight into themselves. Wisdom, self-knowledge, and empathy are the reward for walking a mile in someone's moccasins.

The topsy-turvy customs of Twelvetide no doubt had a similar value. Like body-swap movies, these practices encouraged empathy for the other and were a healthy cautionary reminder that our current roles in life are temporary, so that we had best not get too inflated by them. Finally, they acted as a safety valve, releasing social pressures that had built up over the course of the year from the stresses and strains of the various roles we play. Perhaps for the good of the nation, we should take back Twelfth Night.

Chapter Thirteen

KEEP GOING: EPIPHANY, PLOUGH MONDAY, AND GROUNDHOG DAY

When does the Christmas season end? There is no clear answer to this seemingly simple question. For most Americans it seems to end about halfway through Christmas Day itself, after the last present has been opened or when the credits roll at the end of "It's a Wonderful Life." On the other hand, as we saw in the last chapter, in medieval and early modern Europe the festivities were just getting started on Christmas Day and would not end until Epiphany (January 6). And since for most of its history the Feast of Epiphany was celebrated as an octave (eight days), some would extend the celebration to January 13. In Sweden and Norway, January 13, which is St. Knut's Day, is time for one last party before the Christmas decorations come down: "Twentieth day Knut, Driveth Yule out," as the old saying has it.[1] In the Philippines, Christmastide ends on January 9 with a spectacular procession and day-long celebration of the Feast of the Black Nazarene, a seventeenth-century black wood statue of Jesus carrying the cross. And because of some stubborn hold-outs who refused to accept the reformed calendar of Pope Gregory XIII in 1582, southwest England observes Twelfth Night on January 17, the date determined by the old Julian calendar.

Finally, some folks insist that the season lasts forty days, beginning on December 25 and ending on February 2, the Feast of the Purification of the Blessed Virgin Mary. Hence the Robert Herrick poem that commands Christmas revelers to put away their holiday decorations on the night of February 1:

> Down with the rosemary, and so
> Down with the bays and mistletoe;
> Down with the holly, ivy, all,
> Wherewith ye dress'd the Christmas Hall.[2]

Even if all good things must come to an end, we sympathize with the impulse to keep the merriment going. Here are a few ways to do that.

EPIPHANY, JANUARY 6

For many Christians, the great Feast of the Epiphany is a holy day of obligation, requiring attendance at a religious service. "Epiphany" is the Greek word for manifestation, referring to Christ's manifestation of Himself as the Son of God. Initially, the feast celebrated the manifestation of Jesus at His birth, but when December 25 became the feast for His nativity, January 6 came to focus on three other manifestations: the manifestation of Christ to the Magi, the first manifestation of Christ's miraculous power at the Wedding of Cana, and the manifestation of Christ's sonship when He was baptized by St. John in the Jordan River.

Of these three, the manifestation to the Magi takes center stage for most Protestants and Catholics (among Eastern Christians, it is Christ's baptism). The idea is that when God sent angels to the (Jewish) shepherds to tell them to worship His Son in the manger, He was signifying that the Messiah was for His Chosen People, and when He sent a star to guide the Magi to His Son, He was signifying that the Messiah was for the Gentiles as well. That's good news, especially if you don't have any Jewish blood.

The Magi were a highly esteemed class of priestly scholars from Zoroastrianism, a monotheistic religion that originated in Persia. The Gospels do not specify how many Magi there were or from where they started their journey, but over time tradition added much to their story. The Magi are called the Three Kings in accordance with two Old Testament prophecies that describe kings from Tharsis, Arabia, and Sheba bringing presents to the Messiah (Psalm 71:10) such as gold and frankincense (Issaiah 60:3–6). In the early Middle Ages in the West, the three Wise Men were given names: Melchior, who was old and white-haired and gave gold to the newborn king; Gaspar or Caspar, who was young and ruddy and gave frankincense; and Balthasar, who was black and offered myrrh. In later depictions, Melchior was represented as a European, Caspar as an Asian, and Balthazar as an African—symbolizing the manifestation of the Christ to the peoples of all three continents of the Old World. But according to one ancient tradition, the Magi returned home safely to present-day Iraq and Iran, and decades later, St. Thomas the Apostle, who was evangelizing the area, met them, baptized them, and made them bishops.

PROCLAMATION OF FEASTS

We take calendars for granted, but in former ages it was not so. Early Christians relied on the calculations of scholars from Alexandria (considered the most competent) to determine the date of Easter, which falls on the first Sunday after the first full moon on or after March 21, which is the latest date on which the vernal equinox can occur. Those calculations would be solemnly announced on the Feast of the Epiphany, which was a sensible choice. The feast celebrates an astronomical event, and it is not far from the seasons of Lent and Easter.

MAGI PLAYS

Did you know that theater in the Western world died out in ancient Greece and Rome and was brought back to life by the worship of the Church? The earliest medieval plays began as theatrical reenactments of Gospel passages of the day (Easter, Good Friday, and so forth). Epiphany had an "Office of the Star," which was tied to the liturgy of the feast and was staged in the sanctuary of the church. Over time it grew out of hand: the character Herod was portrayed as a raging lunatic, overthrowing furniture and beating clergy and laity alike with a wooden stick. Church officials decided to ban the play from the sanctuary, at which point it moved outside and became a popular entertainment. William Shakespeare remembered these plays from his childhood, before they were banned by England's Protestant leaders. In *Hamlet*, the young prince complains about overacting that "out-Herods Herod" (III.ii.13). Tamer versions of the medieval Epiphany play continue to exist in the German tradition of *Sternsingen* and the Spanish tradition of the festival of *Los Tres Rejes*.

THE BLESSING OF HOMES

An even older custom is the blessing of homes on the Feast of the Epiphany. A priest may come to the house, sprinkle each room with holy water, and incense it. But the more common practice is the blessing of the house with chalk. At church, the priest blesses chalk and sprinkles it with holy water, saying:

> Bless, O Lord God, this creature chalk, that it may be salutary for mankind; and, through the invocation of Thy most holy name, grant that whoever obtains some of it or writes with it upon the doors of their home the names of Thy saints, Caspar, Melchior and Balthasar, may, through their intercession and merits, receive health of body and protection of soul. Through Christ our Lord. Amen.

The faithful then take the chalk home with them and write on the lintel of their doors the current year along with the letters C, M, and B, interspersed by crosses: 20+C+M+B+23.

Because it is a product of clay, chalk is a fitting symbol for the human nature assumed by the Word whose Incarnation we celebrate this season. The number signifies the years that have elapsed since the Savior's birth into human history, the crosses represent Christ Himself and the holiness of the Magi, and the letters represent the initials of the three kings: Caspar, Melchior, and Balthasar. These same letters can also stand for *Christus mansionem benedicat*—May Christ bless this house.

Blessing the home on Epiphany is appropriate. Just as the Wise Men visited the temporary home of the Infant Jesus and brought Him gifts of gold, frankincense, and myrrh (symbols of His kingship, divinity, and burial), so too do we pray that Christ may visit our temporary (earthly) home with gifts of grace and peace for ourselves and our guests.

EPIPHANY CAROLS

People are (or at least used to be) still in a caroling mood on Epiphany. One noteworthy custom is the star carol. From the fourteenth century to the Reformation, groups would go from house to house holding the Star of Bethlehem and announcing through song that they were the Magi telling of their adventures. The custom, which was a simplified form of the medieval Epiphany play, still exists in Austria and Bavaria (where it is called *Stemsingen*) and in Slavic countries.

We suspect that the author of the most popular Epiphany carol in the English language and perhaps the world was aware of this tradition. John Henry Hopkins Jr. was rector of Christ Episcopal Church in Williamsport, Pennsylvania, and the music teacher at the General Theological Seminary in New York City. For his final year of teaching at the seminary (1857), he wrote "We Three Kings" for a Christmas pageant they were having. Hopkins wrote both the music and the lyrics for the song which, as you can tell from our chapter on Christmas carols (Chapter Nine), was rare: usually, the lyrics were written by one person and the tune by another. The carol also holds the honor of being the first Christmas-Epiphany carol from the United States achieving world-wide popularity: even the British and the French like it. The song aptly impersonates all three kings in the first verse, Melchior in the second, Balthasar in the third, and Caspar in the fourth, while the chorus praises the Christmas Star. By the time the carol is over, the singer or hearer knows who the three kings are, what gifts they brought, and what deeper meaning the gifts have. Written in the distinctive Aeolian mode, it smacks of music from the Middle Ages and Middle East. The first verse is:

> We three kings of Orient are;
> Bearing gifts we traverse afar,
> Field and fountain,
> Moor and mountain,
> Following yonder star.

GIFT-GIVING

In Italy and Spanish-speaking countries, Epiphany rather than Christmas is the occasion for exchanging gifts. In Italy, the old woman Befana brings the presents; in Spanish-speaking countries, it is the Magi (see Chapter Six).

Some cultures split the difference and exchange gifts on both Christmas and Epiphany. In French Canada,

Epiphany was nicknamed "Little Christmas." The practice of opening presents over a period of days makes sense, since children who open all their gifts in a mad frenzy on Christmas morning often become unappreciative and lethargic afterwards.

BLESSING OF WATER

As we mentioned at the beginning of this chapter, Epiphany also celebrates the Baptism of Jesus in the Jordan, which according to Catholic and Orthodox belief is the moment when Christ sanctified water, making it capable of communicating the grace of the sacrament of baptism. It is therefore customary to bless water on this day. The Roman Catholic Church has a traditional and elaborate blessing of water that takes place on the eve of Epiphany and requires, among other things, several exorcisms and infusing the water with a little salt.

Other Christian churches use this occasion to bless natural bodies of water. In the Holy Land, the River Jordan is blessed, and then thousands plunge themselves into the water three times to receive a blessing. In Egypt, the same thing traditionally happens in the Nile; locals also lead their domestic animals into the river for a blessing and dip their religious objects into the river for the same reason. In Greece, this custom is so popular that Epiphany is called *Fota*, the "Blessing of the Waters." After the priest blesses a body of water, he throws a cross into it. The men of the town then compete to retrieve it;

the one who succeeds has good luck for the year. And as we saw in Chapter Seven, the Blessing of the Water has the added advantage of driving away the Christmas demons. The Greeks use the occasion to bless their boats and ships.

FOOD AND DRINK

The signature food for Epiphany (or, sometimes, the night before) is King Cake (also known as Three Kings Cake). A small object is put in a cake. Traditionally, it was a coin; more recently, it is a small figurine of the Infant Jesus. Whoever finds the object in his piece of the cake is king of the merry party—and, at least in New Orleans, where numerous and differently flavored King Cakes are eaten throughout the entire Mardi Gras season, which lasts from Twelfth Night until Mardi Gras (French for "Fat Tuesday"), the day before Lent begins on Ash Wednesday—has to buy the next King Cake. In Austria, Germany, France, England, and Canada, the King Cake contained both a bean and a pea; finding the bean made one a king while the pea made one a queen. In England, an entire court would then be chosen, with each person drawing the name of a character from a hat and assuming that role for the rest of the night.

There was also an element of charity to these celebrations. In France a piece of cake was put aside "for our Lord" and given to a poor person. Another French tradition required each person to pay for his piece of cake. The money collected, called "the gold of the Magi," would be given to the poor or to help pay for the education of a promising but disadvantaged youth.[3]

In Mexico, *Rosca de Reyes* or Kings' Day Bread is a wreath-shaped loaf with cinnamon, anise seed, vanilla extract, and dried fruit. The dinner guest who finds the Baby Jesus in his slice must make the tamales for the next gathering. A similar custom exists in Spain. *Roscón de Reyes* is a delicious cream-filled oval pastry with a hidden bean and a surprise. Whoever finds the surprise gets good luck for the year; whoever finds the bean has to buy the next roscón.

THE DAY AFTER EPIPHANY, JANUARY 7

There is an old English superstition that for every Christmas decoration still up after Epiphany, a single goblin will come into the home. Despite the possible provocation, many wait until the day after Epiphany to pack up the Christmas décor. There is also a tradition of burning the Christmas tree, either piecemeal in the fireplace or intact at some outdoor location. One family we know of in the frozen north (Minnesota) goes out onto the ice, drills a hole in it, inserts the bottom of the tree into the hole, and sets the tree alight. Whatever your method, it would not be inappropriate to sing a last Christmas carol as the tree goes up in flames, and to make this an annual family tradition.

Others find more practical uses for the Christmas tree. Some municipalities have recycling programs that convert Christmas trees into mulch or compost. Others collect trees and throw them into nearby lakes to make fish habitats. In ice-fishing regions, old Christmas trees are used as landmarks on large, frozen lakes (we suppose they eventually end up in the lake as well).

PLOUGH MONDAY, THE MONDAY AFTER

EPIPHANY

In some parts of England, the Monday after the Twelve Days of Christmas is known as Plough Monday, the time to say goodbye to Christmas merriment and return to the grindstone—or desk, or plow, or desk or whatever. Note-worthy customs for the day include blackening one's face, dragging around a decorated plough, and shouting "Penny for the ploughboys!" The blackface is meant to obscure one's identity with soot rather than to mimic another race; still, we do not advise trying out this custom.

Plough Monday is also the occasion for "molly dancing," a form of English Morris dance that involves a troupe of male dancers, one of whom—the "molly" or milquetoast—is attired as a woman. For some, cross-dressing on Twelfth Night just isn't enough (see Chapter Twelve).

CANDLEMAS, FEBRUARY 2

In the modern Catholic and Anglican calendars, February 2 is the Feast of the Presentation of Jesus Christ; in the Byzantine Rite of the Eastern Orthodox and Eastern Catholic Churches, it is the Meeting of the Lord. But for most of the Roman Catholic Church's history, February 2 was the Feast of the Purification of the Blessed Virgin Mary. All three feasts highlight something that took place when Mary and Joseph brought Jesus to the Holy Temple forty days after His birth (Luke 2:21–40)—February 2 being forty days after December 25. The new Catholic and Anglican Feast of the Presentation recalls that Jesus, a firstborn male, was "redeemed" or consecrated to the Lord in conformity with the Mosaic Law.[4] The Byzantine feast focuses on the meeting of Simeon and Anna with the long-awaited Messiah. And the old Roman Catholic feast emphasized that Mary presented herself at the Temple to be ritually purified from childbirth according to the Law of Moses.

KEEPING THE CANDLES IN CANDLEMAS

The Feast of the Purification is nicknamed Candlemas ("Candle Mass") because in the Middle Ages the day was marked by a blessing of candles and a procession after Mass. Having a light-themed ceremony is an appropriate way to end the Christmas season (if indeed Candlemas is the end of the Christmas season!), and it ties in well with Simeon's epithet of Jesus as a Light to the Revelation of the Gentiles (Luke 2:32). According to saints such as Anselm of Canterbury, candles are an excellent symbol for Christ. The wax, made from the "virginal bee," signifies the pure flesh of Our Lord taken from His mother, the wick symbolizes His human soul, and the flame represents His divinity.

Candles blessed on Candlemas Day are taken home and used throughout the year as a "sacramental," an object set apart for special use to excite good thoughts, increase devotion, and impart blessings. Special uses for Candlemas candles include protection from storms and the consolation of the sick and dying. In Poland, there is a charming legend that Mary, under the appellation "the Mother of God of the Blessed Thunder Candle" (*Matka Bvska Gromniczna*), wards off hungry wolves.[5]

GROUNDHOG DAY?

Simeon's prophecy and the focus on light also led to a peculiar folk belief that the weather on February 2 had a particularly keen prognostic value. If the sun shone for the greater part of Candlemas, there would be forty more days of winter, but if the skies were cloudy and gray, there would be an early spring. In Germany this lore was elaborated by bringing a badger or a hedgehog into the equation, but when German immigrants arrived in Pennsylvania, they could find none of these creatures around. Instead they saw plenty of what the local Native Americans called a *wojak*—the woodchuck, also known as the groundhog . The Indians considered the groundhog to be a wise animal, and it seemed only natural to appoint the furry fellow "Seer of Seers, Sage of Sages, Prognosticator of

Prognosticators, and Weather Prophet Extraordinary," as they say every year in Punxsutawney, Pennsylvania. So there you have it: Groundhog Day is actually a Christmas custom.

GOODBYE AND HELLO

In some places Candlemas is the time to take down all Christmas decorations, including the nativity scene. All the greenery is burnt—it is bad luck not to, and it is good luck to strew the ashes of Christmas plants over garden and fields. Either the remnants of the Yule log are burnt up on Candlemas, or a piece is reserved in order to start next Christmas's Yule log.

And speaking of the Yule log, as we have seen in England, Candlemas was also the day to pick the Yule log for next Christmas and set it aside to dry.

Chapter Fourteen

PUTTING IT ALL TOGETHER

Congratulations! You have successfully surveyed a vast array of Christmas customs—some beautiful, some bizarre; some ancient, some new; some charming, some disturbing. If you are of a practical frame of mind, your next question is probably, *What do I do with this information?* Besides the obvious answer of boring your friends and relatives with inane Christmas trivia over rounds of eggnog, we recommend actually putting some of these customs back into practice. Here's how.

Delay Your Gratification. If *Why We Kiss under the Mistletoe* shows anything, it is how different the rhythm of the traditional Christmas was from a modern Christmas. The modern Christmas season seems to start earlier and earlier each year and then ends abruptly on Christmas Day or the day after, whereas the traditional Christmas observes the season of Advent as a time of preparation and restraint and then pulls out all the stops for the Twelve Days of Christmas.

We recommend the traditional pattern: it is simply more fun. Use Advent to build anticipation. You don't have to say no to every Christmas party invitation held before December 24. Just find little ways of holding back: Bake Christmas cookies but don't eat them all, avoid the yearly inundation of cheesy holiday music on the airwaves in late November and December, and delay putting up your Christmas tree or Christmas lights (and then keep them up until January 6). Practice suspenseful customs like the Advent calendar or Advent wreath. Then, during the Twelve Days of Christmas, put the pedal to the metal and celebrate with friends and family. We understand that not everyone is able to observe a week and a half of unbroken merriment, as many people must return to work soon after Christmas Day. But we do maintain that it is possible for everyone to keep up a spirit of Christmas cheer for twelve days, if only you have not emptied your tank by December 25.

Finally, it is our experience that delayed gratification is especially good for the children. Stretching out the exchange of gifts over several days, for example, helps them better appreciate what they receive.

Eclectic Is Okay. The customs mentioned in this book hail from different times and places. Most of them are the product of an organic development, where each culture with its own unique ecosystem produces distinctive and harmonious symbols and practices over time. But armed with the knowledge contained in this book, you can combine customs from ancient Rome, medieval France, modern Iceland, and sunny Jamaica.

The result could be a bit of a mismatch, like penguins on a tropical island. But despite the risks involved, we contend that it is okay to be eclectic, within reason. We are, after all, Americans, and one of the secrets of our cultural vitality is our ability to combine or integrate different cultural traditions. Traditionally, this vitality is called the American melting pot, but perhaps a more accurate metaphor is the American salad bowl, where each ingredient retains its flavor and identity but becomes part of a larger delicious unity. Don't be afraid to create your own Christmas salad or stew, so to speak, from different world traditions. Or to use another metaphor, think of yourself as a florist taking different kinds of flowers and plants from around the world and putting them together in a beautiful arrangement.

Don't Overdo It. That said, sometimes less is more. If you try to adopt every Christmas custom you read about in this book, you will go crazy. Pick what looks good for you and your family, and build *gradually* year after year, seeing what works and what doesn't.

Let Your Freak Flag Fly. Have fun with these customs! The ones that have a dark side, for instance, can be particularly memorable. Stir things up by dressing like one of St. Nicholas's demonic sidekicks and then wreak havoc on Santa and his elves when they visit your local mall. Then, run like the devil before the mall cops get you.

Okay, that's probably going too far. But we can say that one year we had St. Nicholas visit our local parish on the eve of his feast day accompanied by an angel and Cert the devil (see Chapter Five), and it was a great success. Our Cert was scary but not too scary, and the children loved it.

You can also take a walk on the wild side with the topsy-turvy customs of the season, such as making the kids the rulers of the day on Childermas (December 28) or hosting a gender-bending party in which men dress like women and vice versa (on Twelfth Night, January 5). As we argue at end of Chapter Twelve, there is value in walking a mile in someone else's moccasins—or high heels.

Be Merry. We have talked about the meaning of merriment in Chapter Eleven, but we have one final thought on the concept.

Reflect for a moment on the difference between "fun" and "merriment." "Fun" implies a form of entertainment that is not necessarily bad but is usually superficial and can typically be enjoyed alone. Perhaps a young man would have more fun playing video games with his friends, but it is conceivable that he can still have some fun playing the game by himself.

"Merriment," on the other hand, necessitates fellowship. People usually do not make merry alone in a room; they make merry at a party or a festival. Merriment presupposes strong community and a truly divine and memorable reason to celebrate: think how absurd it would be to say "Merry Administrative Professionals' Day." But "Merry Christmas" still has meaning, and not just because Christ's Mass is mentioned. When we wish someone to be merry on Our Lord's birthday, we are hoping that they will have more than just a good time. Aren't we invoking a kind of blessing?

Of course, all of this involves risk: there is an obsolete term in English, "merry-drunk," that suggests as much. But as Josef Pieper points out in his work *In Tune with the World: A Theory of Festivity*, all festivity contains "a natural peril and a germ of degeneration" because all festivity carries with it an element of lavishness. But just as lavishness need not involve decadence, "wet" merriment need not involve drowning.

The chief enemies of Christmas are anxiety and stress. The antidote is merriment. There are a million reasons to get annoyed: every kid is disappointed at Christmas, Uncle Bob is sloshed, and Aunt Sally is argumentative or passive aggressive. But we all know the old saw about the glass being half full or half empty. Come into the Christmas season with lowered expectations, and when things go awry choose to look at the bright side. You can do it.

After all, Christmas itself is a gift. It has been given to you. Receive it joyfully.

WORKS CONSULTED

Abruzzi, William S., "When Was Jesus Born? A Critical
    Examination of Jesus' Birth Year As Presented in the
    Infancy Narratives," ResearchGate, January 2016,
    https://www.researchgate.net/publication/334577128_
    When_Was_Jesus_Born_A_Critical_Examination_of_
    Jesus'_Birth_Year_as_Presented_in_the_Infancy_
    Narratives.

Barnett, James H., *The American Christmas* (New York:
    Macmillan, 1954).

Basu, Tanya, "Who is Krampus? Explaining the Horrific
    Christmas Beast," *National Geographic*, December 5,

2018, https://www.nationalgeographic.com/news/2018/12/131217-krampus-christmas-santa-devil/.

Beaulieu, David, "How the Tradition of Kissing Under Mistletoe Started," *The Spruce*, May 15, 2019, https://www.thespruce.com/kissing-under-the-mistletoe-2131215.

Bennett, William J., *The True Saint Nicholas: Why He Matters to Christmas* (Howard Books, 2018).

Benson, Louis F., *Studies of Familiar Hymns*, First Series (Philadelphia: The Westminster Press. 1924).

Bowler, Gerry, *The World Encyclopedia of Christmas* (Toronto: McClelland & Stewart Ltd., 2000).

Bradshaw, Paul F., and Maxwell E. Johnson, *The Origins of Feasts, Fasts, and Seasons in Early Christianity* (Collegeville, Minnesota: Pueblo Press, 2011).

Burton, Katherine, and Helmut Ripperger, *Feast Day Cookbook* (Catholic Authors Press, 2005).

Chesterton, G. K., *Chesterton in Black and White*, ed. Geir Hasnes (Kongsberg, Norway: Classica, 2021).

——————*The Thing* (London: Sheed & Ward, 1929).

Cioffari, Gerardo, *Saint Nicholas: His Life, Miracles and Legends*, trans. Victoria Sportelli (Bari, Italy: Centro Studi Nicolaiani, 2008).

Cole, Helen Rosemary, "Why Is Mistletoe," *The Journal of American Folklore* 59, no. 234 (October–December 1946), 528-529.

Crippen, T. G., *Christmas and Christmas Lore* (London: Blackie and Son Ltd., 1923).

Drury, Susan, "Customs and Beliefs Associated with Christmas Evergreens: A Preliminary Survey," *Folklore*, 98, no. 2 (1987), 194–99.

English, Adam, *The Saint Who Would Be Santa Claus: The True Life and Trials of Nicholas of Myra* (Waco, Texas: Baylor University Press, 2012).

Farmer, David, *Oxford Dictionary of Saints*, 5th ed. (Oxford: Oxford University Press, 2003).

Geisser, David, and Thomas Kelly, *The Vatican Christmas Book* (Manchester, New Hampshire: Sophia Institute Press, 2020).

The Guinness Book of World Records, www. guinnessworldrecords.com.

Herrick, Robert, *Works of Robert Herrick*, vol. 2, ed. Alfred Pollard (London: Lawrence & Bullen, 1891).

"Hogmanay Night," *Ulster Journal of Archaeology*, First Series, vol. 8 (1860), 150.

Jones, W., *Saint Nicholas of Myra, Bari, and Manhattan: Biography of a Legend* (Chicago: University of Chicago Press, 1978).

Kanner, Leo, "Mistletoe, Magic and Medicine," *Bulletin of the History of Medicine* 7, no. 8 (October 1939), 875–936.

Krymow, Vincenzina, *Mary's Flowers: Gardens, Legends, and Meditations* (Cincinnati, Ohio : St. Anthony Messenger Press, 1999).

Lindsay, Maurice, "Auld Lang Syne," *The Burns Encyclopedia*, 3rd ed. (1996), http://www.robertburns. org/encyclopedia/.

Little, Becky, "How Mistletoe Became Everyone's Favorite Parasite," *National Geographic*, https://www. nationalgeographic.com/news/2015/12/151218- mistletoe-christmas-holiday-kissing-parasite-birds- cancer/.

McGinley, Phyllis, *Merry Christmas, Happy New Year* (New York: Viking Press, 1958).

Miles, Clement A., *Christmas in Ritual and Tradition, Christian and Pagan* (London: T. Fisher Unwin, 1912).

"Mistle, n.," and "Mistletoe, n.," etymology, in *Oxford English Dictionary*, 3rd ed. (Oxford University Press, June 2002), https://www-oed-com.ezproxy.baylor.edu/ view/Entry/119966; https://www-oed-com.ezproxy. baylor.edu/view/Entry/120134.

Muir, Frank, *Christmas Customs & Traditions* (New York: Taplinger Publishing Company, 1975).

Nevin, May, "Christmas Customs and Legends," *Irish Monthly* 61, no. 726 (December 1933), 733–36.

The New Oxford Book of Carols, eds. Hugh Keyte, Andrew Parrott, and Clifford Bartlett (Oxford University Press, 1998).

Nothaft, Carl Philipp Emanuel, "From Sukkot to Saturnalia: The Attack on Christmas in Sixteenth-Century Chronological Scholarship," *Journal of the History of Ideas* 72, no. 4 (October 2011), 503–22.

Restad, Penne L., *Christmas in America: A History* (New York: Oxford University Press, 1995).

——————— "Christmas in Nineteenth-Century America," *History Today* 45, no. 12 (December 1, 1995), 13–19.

Ricciotti, Giuseppe, and Ferdinand Prat, *The Mystery of Christmas*, ed. Aloysius Croft (Kansas City, Missouri: Romanitas Press, 2021).

Roll, Susan K., *Toward the Origin of Christmas* (Kampen, Netherlands: Kok Pharos Publishing House, 1995).

Rollins, Hyder E., ed., *Cavalier and Puritan: Ballads and Broadsides Illustrating the Great Rebellion of 1640–1660*, (New York: New York University Press, 1923).

"Saint Nicholas Day (Mikuláš)," myCzechRepublic, http://www.myczechrepublic.com/czech_culture/czech_holidays/saint_nicholas.html.

Simmons, Kurt, "The Origins of Christmas and the Date of Christ's Birth," *Journal of the Evangelical Theology Society* 58, no. 2 (2015), 299–324.

——————— "Revisiting the Fathers: An Examination of the Christmas Date in Several Early Patristic Writers," *Questions Liturgiques* 98 (2017), 143–80.

Snyder, Phillip V., *The Christmas Tree Book: The History of the Christmas Tree and Antique Christmas Tree Ornaments* (New York: Viking Press, 1976).

Stephenson, Kristen, "Seven Six Flags Amusement Parks Set a Romantic Mistletoe Kissing World Record," Guinness World Records, December 12, 2016, https://www.guinnessworldrecords.com/news/2016/12/seven-six-flags-amusement-parks-set-a-romantic-mistletoe-filled-world-record-455044.

Stevens, Patricia Bunning, *Merry Christmas! A History of the Holiday* (New York: Macmillan, 1979).

Tighe, William J., "Calculating Christmas," *Touchstone* 16, no. 10 (December 2003), https://www.touchstonemag.com/archives/article.php?id=16-10-012-v.

Vitz, Evelyn Birge, *A Continual Feast: A Cookbook to Celebrate the Joys of Family and Faith throughout the Christian Year* (San Francisco: Ignatius Press, 1985).

Walsh, Michael, *Butler's Lives of Patron Saints* (Tunbridge Wells, England: Burns and Oates, 1987).

Waugh, Evelyn, *Helena* (London: Chapman & Hall, 1960).

Weiser, Francis X., *The Christmas Book* (New York: Harcourt, Brace, and Co., 1952).

———————— *Handbook of Christian Feasts and Customs: The Year of the Lord in Liturgy and Folklore* (New York: Harcourt, Brace & World, Inc., 1958).

——————— *Religious Customs in the Family: The Radiation of the Liturgy into Christian Homes* (Collegeville, Minnesota: Liturgical Press, 1956).

Wernecke, Herbert H., *Christmas Customs around the World* (Philadelphia: Westminster Press, 1959).

Notes

Introduction

1. "Christmas," *The Aldine*, vol. 4, no. 12 (December 1871), 184.

Chapter One: Christmas's Roller Coaster Past

1. The angel implicitly commands Joseph to adopt Jesus when he tells him to name Mary's son "Jesus," an act that only a father would perform (see Matthew 1:21).

2. For a summary of the criticism, see William S. Abruzzi, "When Was Jesus Born? A Critical

Examination of Jesus' Birth Year as Presented in the
Infancy Narratives," ResearchGate, January 2016,
https://www.researchgate.net/publication/334577128
_When_Was_Jesus_Born_A_Critical_Examination
_of_Jesus'_Birth_Year_as_Presented_in_the_Infancy
_Narratives. And among the skeptics, see especially
Raymond Brown, *The Birth of the Messiah: A
Commentary on the Infancy Narratives in the Gospels
of Matthew and Luke*, new updated ed. (New York,
London: Yale University Press, 1993), 22 : "I suggest
that Matthew did not draw upon an account of
historical events but rewrote a pre-Matthean narrative
associating the birth of Jesus, son of Joseph, with the
patriarch Joseph and the birth of Moses." Wendy
Cotter, on the other hand, has shown that only a small
portion of the infancy narrative in Matthew and Luke
pertains to the supernatural (the Virgin Birth, the visit
of the angels, and so forth). Most of the material
concerns mundane facts of the events, e.g., the census,
the identity and actions of political figures, the details
of Mary and Joseph's travel and the accommodations
for the birth, and the like. If the narratives are
mythologized, or "built upon the Moses story," it is
striking that so little of these materials reflects those
concerns (see *Miracles in Greco-Roman Antiquity: A
Sourcebook for the Study of New Testament Miracle
Stories* {London: Routledge, 1999}). Cotter's extensive
bibliography covers ancient primary sources as well as
monographs and essays on the topic.

3. For most of these points, see Kurt Simmons, "The Origins of Christmas and the Date of Christ's Birth," *Journal of the Evangelical Theology Society* 58, no. 2 (2015): 299–324.

4. The ancient Biblical approach known as *tupos*, or "Biblical typology" is a deeply rooted Jewish interpretation. It is an intertextual approach that focuses on thematic parallels between two texts, one earlier, the other later. According to this approach, the original text is a foundational "type" upon which the later text, the "antitype" is paralleled. A clear example is the Bronze Serpent that Moses "lifted up" in the wilderness in Numbers chapter 22 to heal the snake-bitten Israelites, which is a "type" of Christ on the Cross: Jesus, speaking to Nicodemus about that Old Testament passage, explains in John chapter 3 that the Son of Man must likewise be "lifted up" (on the Cross). Here is a case in which the Evangelist clearly drew on an earlier Biblical text. But far from impugning the historical accuracy of the New Testament account, this kind of intertextuality signals the deeper meaning of the Gospel narrative in a "how much more" (*qal wahomer*) sort of way.

5. Paul F. Bradshaw and Maxwell E. Johnson, *The Origins of Feasts, Fasts, and Seasons in Early Christianity* (Collegeville, Minnesota: Pueblo Press, 2011), 123–25, 131.

6. See William J. Tighe, "Calculating Christmas," *Touchstone* 16, no. 10 (December 2003), https://

www.touchstonemag.com/archives/article.php?id=16
-10-012-v.

7. Ibid.

8. See Simmons, "The Origins of Christmas" and
   Bradshaw and Johnson, *The Origins of Feasts, 126.*

9. See Simmons, "The Origins of Christmas."

10. See Augustine, *On the Trinity 4.4.7–5.9.*

11. *The Thomason Tracts* (669. f. 10 (47)), dated April 8,
    1646, reprinted in *Cavalier and Puritan: Ballads and
    Broadsides Illustrating the Great Rebellion of 1640–
    1660*, ed. Hyder E. Rollins (New York: New York
    University Press, 1923), 161.

12. A Christmas song from *Poor Robin's Almanack*
    (1695). See Weiser, *Christmas Book, 47.*

13. See Christopher Klein, "When Massachusetts Banned
    Christmas," History.com, December 21, 2020, https://
    www.history.com/news/when-massachusetts-banned-
    christmas;new and Francis X. Weiser, *The Christmas
    Book* (New York: Harcourt, Brace, and Co., 1952), 48.

14. See Penne Restad, "Christmas in Nineteenth-Century
    America," *History Today* 45, no. 12 (December 1,
    1995): 13–19.

15. Ibid., 19.

CHAPTER TWO: THE BUILDUP

1. See "Largest Advent Calendar," Guinness World
   Records, https://www.guinnessworldrecords.com

/world-records/largest-advent-calendar and "Most Valuable Advent Calendar," Guinness World Records, https://www.guinnessworldrecords.com/world-records/most-valuable-advent-calendar-.

2. Maria Trapp, *Around the Year with the Trapp Family* (New York: Pantheon, 1955), 16.

3. "Advent in Mariazell," Hotel Haus Franzikus, http://www.haus-franziskus.at/advent-mariazell.

4. "The World's Largest Advent Wreath Is in Saint-Gall, Switzerland," FSSPX News, December 15, 2017, https://fsspx.news/en/news-events/news/world%E2%80%99s-largest-advent-wreath-saint-gall-switzerland-34342.

5. "World's Largest Advent Wreath Damaged—Police Looking for Perpetrators," DE24News, December 6, 2020, https://www.de24.news/en/2020/12/worlds-largest-advent-wreath-damaged-police-looking-for-perpetrators.html.

6. Von Trapp, *Around the Year*, 45.

7. Meghan Keneally, "See the Biggest Live Nativity Scene in the World," ABC News, December 2, 2014, https://abcnews.go.com/US/biggest-live-nativity-scene-world/story?id=27307510.

8. J-P Mauro, "The World's Smallest Nativity Scene Is Microscopic," Aleteia, December 7, 2020, https://aleteia.org/2020/12/07/the-worlds-smallest-nativity-scene-is-microscopic/.

9. "Largest Nativity Scene Figures," Guinness World Records, https://www.guinnessworldrecords.com /world-records/largest-nativity-scene-figures

10. "French Town Hopes to Break Record with Huge Christmas Creche," Associated Press, December 1, 2017, https://apnews.com/article/facf566861604233ae 4734c4511835c6.

11. On both Sundays in the traditional Catholic Mass and on the Last Sunday before Advent in the Anglican and Episcopal Churches.

12. See Katherine Burton and Helmut Ripperger, *Feast Day Cookbook* (Philadelphia: David McKay Company, Inc., 1951), 168–69.; Von Trapp, *Around the Year*, 33; Helen McLoughlin, *Family Advent Customs* (Collegeville, Minnesota: Liturgical Press, 1954), 8; and Evelyn Birge Vitz, *A Continual Feast: A Cookbook to Celebrate the Joys of Family and Faith Throughout the Christian Year* (San Francisco: Ignatius Press, 1985), 152–53; Nigella Lawson, "Ultimate Christmas Pudding," https:// www.nigella.com/recipes/ultimate-christmas-pudding.

13. *The Liturgical Year* (Great Falls, Montana: St. Bonaventure Publications, 2000), 1:494–95.

14. "Thomasing, n.," *Oxford English Dictionary*.

15. Francis X. Weiser, *Handbook of Christian Feasts and Customs* (New York: Harcourt, Brace, and World, 1958), 58.

16. Providentially, St. Ephrem the Syrian had described St.
    Thomas as a "dawn dispelling India's darkness."
    Though no one is certain, it is possible that Thomas
    died on the winter solstice and that this fact inspired
    Ephrem's verse. Another possibility is the reverse: that
    the verse inspired the placement of the feast on the
    winter solstice.

17. This account of the European customs surrounding St.
    Thomas's Day is taken from the *Encyclopedia of
    Christmas and New Year's Celebrations*, 2nd ed.
    (Omnigraphics, 2003).

CHAPTER THREE: THE REAL ST. NICK

1. "Nicholas, St," *Oxford Dictionary of the Christian
    Church*, 3rd ed., eds. F. L. Cross and E. A. Livingstone
    (Oxford: Oxford University Press, 1997), 1148.

2. Adam English, *The Saint Who Would Be Santa
    Claus: The True Life and Trials of Nicholas of Myra*
    (Waco, Texas: Baylor University Press, 2012), 58.

3. Ibid., 93.

4. Earlier scholarship was skeptical of Nicholas's
    attendance at the Council, but more recent work
    contends that it was probable (see English, *The Saint
    Who Would Be Santa Claus*, 13; Gerardo Cioffari,
    Saint Nicholas: His Life, Miracles and Legends, trans.
    Victoria Sportelli {Bari: Centro Studi Nicolaiani,
    2008}, 9, 41).

5. English, *The Saint Who Would Be Santa Claus*, 108.

6. Sulpicius Severus, *Gallus* book 3, chapter 6, paragraph 3.

7. English, *The Saint Who Would Be Santa Claus*, 122.

8. Ibid., 151.

9. Michael Walsh, *Butler's Lives of Patron Saints* (Tunbridge Wells, England: Burns and Oates, 1987), 350.

10. English, *The Saint Who Would Be Santa Claus*, 167.

11. Ibid., 184.

12. Ibid., 14.

13. Ibid., 16.

14. Ibid., 3.

15. Ibid., 14.

CHAPTER FOUR: APPLE-CHEEKED TRANSFORMATION

1. Francis X. Weiser, *Handbook of Christian Feasts and Customs: The Year of the Lord in Liturgy and Folklore* (New York: Harcourt, Brace & World, Inc., 1958), 132.

2. Adam English, *The Saint Who Would Be Santa Claus: The True Life and Trials of Nicholas of Myra* (Waco, Texas: Baylor University Press, 2012), 88.

3. Charles W. Jones, *Saint Nicholas of Myra, Bari, and Manhattan: Biography of a Legend* (Chicago: University of Chicago Press, 1978), 303.

4. Weiser, *Handbook*, 133.

5. Ibid., 340.

6. Clement Miles, *Christmas in Ritual and Tradition, Christian and Pagan* (London: T. Fisher Unwin, 1912), 36.

7. Francis X. Weiser, *Religious Customs in the Family* (Collegeville, Minnesota: Liturgical Press, 1956), 41–42.

8. Francis X. Weiser, *The Christmas Book* (New York: Harcourt, Brace, and Co., 1952), 163–64.

9. Weiser, *Handbook*, 113

10. Edwin G. Burrows, and Mike Wallace, *Gotham: A History of New York City to 1898* (New York: Oxford University Press, 1999), 462–63. Moore, incidentally, wrote the poem simply to entertain his children. When they encouraged him to publish it, he did so on condition of anonymity; as a respected Episcopalian professor of Biblical studies and ancient languages at the General Theological Seminary in New York City, he was worried about his professional reputation. Moore eventually owned up to his authorship in 1844.

11. See Weiser, *Handbook*, 113.

12. Ibid.

13. David Farmer, on the other hand, alleges that St. Nicholas was melded with "Nordic folkloric legends of a magician who both punished naughty children and rewarded good ones with presents" [emphasis

added]. David Farmer, *Oxford Dictionary of Saints*, 5th ed. (Oxford: Oxford University Press, 2003), 386.

14. Charles W. Jones, *Saint Nicholas of Myra, Bari, and Manhattan: Biography of a Legend* (Chicago: University of Chicago Press, 1978), 315.

15. Phyllis McGinley, *Merry Christmas, Happy New Year* (New York: Viking Press, 1958), 15.

16. G. K. Chesterton, *Chesterton in Black and White*, ed. Geir Hasnes (Kongsberg, Norway: Classica, 2021), 64.

CHAPTER FIVE: THE GOOD, THE BAD, AND THE UGLY

1. Clement Miles, *Christmas in Ritual and Tradition, Christian and Pagan* (London: T. Fisher Unwin, 1912), 47.

2. Michell Zappa, "Portrait of Sinterklaas and Zwarte Piet," Wikimedia Commons, https://commons. wikimedia.org/wiki/File:Sinterklaas_zwarte_piet.jpg. This photograph is reproduced cropped, under the Attribution–ShareAlike 2.0 Generic Creative Commons License: https://creativecommons.org/ licenses/by-sa/2.0/legalcode.

3. Gerry Bowler, *The World Encyclopedia of Christmas* (Toronto: McClelland & Stewart Ltd., 2000), 103.

4. A *fouet* is a birch rod.

5. "Who Travels with St. Nicholas," St. Nicholas Center, https://www.stnicholascenter.org/around-the-world/who-travels-with-st-nicholas.

6. Gerry Bowler, *The World Encyclopedia of Christmas* (Toronto: McClelland & Stewart Ltd., 2000), 74.

7. *Harper's Weekly*, December 26, 1857, 820–21.

CHAPTER SIX: SANTA'S COMPETITION

1. Charles W. Jones, *Saint Nicholas of Myra, Bari, and Manhattan: Biography of a Legend* (Chicago: University of Chicago Press, 1978), 313.

2. Baltica, "The Gävle Goat," Wikimedia Commons, https://commons.wikimedia.org/wiki/File:Christmas-Goat.JPG.

3. "Christmas His Masque," in Ben Jonson, *The Complete Masques*, ed. Stephen Orgel (New Haven, Connecticut: Yale, 1969), 233.

4. W. E. S. Ralston, *The Songs of the Russian People* (London: Ellis and Green, 1872), 187–88.

5. Gerry Bowler, *The World Encyclopedia of Christmas* (Toronto: McClelland & Stewart Ltd., 2000), 91.

CHAPTER SEVEN: COME TO THE DARK SIDE

1. Francis X. Weiser, *Handbook of Christian Feasts and Customs: The Year of the Lord in Liturgy and*

Folklore (New York: Harcourt, Brace & World, Inc., 1958), 124.

2. William Shakespeare, *Hamlet* I.i.158–64.

3. "Sain, v.," 1a, *Oxford English Dictionary.*

4. Weiser, *Handbook*, 58.

5. Katherine Burton and Helmut Ripperger, *Feast Day Cookbook* (1951; repr. Catholic Authors Press, 2005), 170.

6. Gerry Bowler, *The World Encyclopedia of Christmas* (Toronto: McClelland & Stewart Ltd., 2000), 197.

7. Clement Miles, *Christmas in Ritual and Tradition, Christian and Pagan* (London: T. Fisher Unwin, 1912), 246.

8. Gerry Bowler, *The World Encyclopedia of Christmas* (Toronto: McClelland & Stewart Ltd., 2000), 123.

9. Ibid., 135.

10. Ibid., 246.

11. Ibid., 248.

CHAPTER EIGHT: DECKING THE HALLS

1. "Christmas," *The Aldine* 4, no. 12 (December 1871): 184.

2. Vincenzina Krymow, *Mary's Flowers: Gardens, Legends, and Meditations* (Cincinnati: St. Anthony Messenger Press, 1999), 48.

3. Francis X. Weiser, *The Christmas Book* (New York: Harcourt, Brace, and Co., 1952), 121.

4. Gerry Bowler, *The World Encyclopedia of Christmas* (Toronto: McClelland & Stewart Ltd., 2000), 119.

5. Tertullian, *On Idolatry*, chapter 15.

6. See "Baccalaureate," Online Etymology Dictionary, https://www.etymonline.com.

7. Evelyn Waugh, *Helena* (London: Chapman & Hall, 1960), 15–16.

8. Pliny the Elder, *Natural History*, book 16, chapter 95.

9. "Hogmanay Night," *Ulster Journal of Archaeology, First Series*, vol. 8 (1860), 150.

10. Francis X. Weiser, *Handbook of Christian Feasts and Customs: The Year of the Lord in Liturgy and Folklore* (New York: Harcourt, Brace & World, Inc., 1958), 104.

11. David Beaulieu, "How the Tradition of Kissing under Mistletoe Started," The Spruce, May 15, 2019, https://www.thespruce.com/kissing-under-the-mistletoe-2131215; Leo Kanner, "Mistletoe, Magic and Medicine," *Bulletin of the History of Medicine* 7, no. 8 (October 1939): 875–936; Becky Little, "How Mistletoe Became Everyone's Favorite Parasite," *National Geographic*, https://www.nationalgeographic.com/news/2015/12/151218-mistletoe-christmas-holiday-kissing-parasite-birds-cancer/.

12. Adapted from Helen Rosemary Cole, "Why Is Mistletoe," *The Journal of American Folklore* 59, no. 234 (October–December 1946): 528–29.

13. T. G. Crippen, *Christmas and Christmas Lore* (London: Blackie and Son Ltd, 1923), 24.

14. "Most Couples Kissing under the Mistletoe, (Multiple Venues)," Guinness World Records, https://www .guinnessworldrecords.com/world-records/449086 -most-couples-kissing-under-the-mistletoe-multiple -venues; "Most Couples Kissing under the Mistletoe," Guinness World Records, https://www .guinnessworldrecords.com/world-records/103559 -most-couples-kissing-under-the-mistletoe-single -venue.

15. Kristen Stephenson, "Seven Six Flags Amusement Parks Set a Romantic Mistletoe Kissing World Record," Guinness World Records, December 12, 2016, https://www.guinnessworldrecords.com/news /2016/12/seven-six-flags-amusement-parks-set -a-romantic-mistletoe-filled-world-record-455044.

16. Poor Robin, "A Christmas Song" of 1695, cited in William Sandys, *Christmastide: Its History, Festivities, and Carols* (London: John Russell Smith, 1852), 128.

CHAPTER NINE: NOT-SO-SILENT NIGHT

1. "The Story Behind 'The Christmas Song,'" NPR, December 25, 2017, https://web.archive.org/web

/20200523021136/https://www.npr.org/transcripts
/572408088.

2.   From the office of Matins; translation mine.

3.   Quoted in Dan Evon and David Mikkelson, "Was
      'Jingle Bells' Written as a Christmas Song?" Snopes,
      December 16, 2014, https://www.snopes.com/fact
      -check/jingle-bells-thanksgiving-carol/.

4.   Louis F. Benson, *Studies of Familiar Hymns, First
      Series* (Philadelphia: The Westminster Press, 1924), 5.

5.   Robert L. May, "Robert May Tells How Rudolph, the
      Red-Nosed Reindeer, Came into Being," *The
      Gettysburg Times*, December 22, 1975, 16.

CHAPTER TEN: WASSAIL!

1.   Clement Miles, *Christmas in Ritual and Tradition,
      Christian and Pagan* (London: T. Fisher Unwin, 1912),
      283.

2.   For the meals of Italy, Mexico, and Provence, see
      Evelyn Birge Vitz, *A Continual Feast: A Cookbook to
      Celebrate the Joys of Family and Faith throughout the
      Christian Year* (San Francisco: Ignatius Press, 1985),
      125–32.

3.   Mike Janela, "Largest Gingerbread House for Charity
      Gets Us in the Christmas Spirit," Guinness World
      Records, December 11, 2013, https://
      www.guinnessworldrecords.com/news/2013/12

/largest-gingerbread-house-for-charity-gets-us-in-the
-christmas-spirit-53612.

4. "The Candy Cane Is Catholic," *Faith & Family* (December 2001): 58; Webb Garrison, *Treasury of Christmas Stories* (Nashville: Rutledge Hill Press, 1990).

5. Lucile Saunders McDonald, *Swan among the Indians: Life of James G. Swan, 1818–1900; Based upon Swan's Hitherto Unpublished Diaries and Journals* (Hillsboro, Oregon: Binford & Mort: 1972), 99.

6. See "Mull, v. 2," OED Online, https://www-oed-com .ezproxy.baylor.edu/view/Entry/123463?rskey=eC9GC u&result=13&isAdvanced=false.

7. Robert Herrick, *Works of Robert Herrick*, Alfred Pollard, ed. (London: Lawrence & Bullen, 1891), 2:145–46.

CHAPTER ELEVEN: LOOKING A LOT LIKE CHRISTMAS

1. G. K. Chesterton, "The Spirit of Christmas" in *The Thing* (London: Sheed & Ward, 1929), 251.

2. Ibid., 252.

3. Francis X. Weiser, *Handbook of Christian Feasts and Customs* (New York: Harcourt, Brace, and World, 1958), 68.

4. Ibid., 74–75.

5. Gerry Bowler, *The World Encyclopedia of Christmas* (Toronto: McClelland & Stewart Ltd., 2000), 242.

6. Ibid., 9.

7. Weiser, *Handbook*, 72.

8. Ibid., 109–10.

9. E. E. Reynolds, *St. John Fisher* (Post Falls, Idaho: Mediatrix Press, 1955), 332.

10. Weiser, *Handbook*, 69.

11. Melissa Mohr, "'Merry' vs. 'Happy' Christmas," *Christian Science Monitor*, December 20, 2018, https://www.csmonitor.com/The-Culture/In-a-Word /2018/1220/Merry-versus-Happy-Christmas.

12. Bowler, *World Encyclopedia*, 243.

13. Ibid., 242.

14. Ibid., 255.

15. Robert Herrick, "Ceremonies for Christmas," All Poetry, https://allpoetry.com/ Ceremonies-For-Christmas.

CHAPTER TWELVE: THE TOPSY-TURVY TWELVE DAYS OF CHRISTMAS

1. Acts 6:5–7:59.

2. "What Are the Origins of the Christmas Dinner?" Frequently Asked Questions, National Defence and the Canadian Forces, November 1, 2011, http://

www.cmp-cpm.forces.gc.ca/dhh-dhp/faq/index-eng.asp?cat=hertra&FaqID=87.

3. Thomas More, *A Dialogue Concerning Heresies*, 261.

4. A recipe for one such treat, the Polish *podkovy*, can be found in Evelyn Vitz's *A Continual Feast* (San Francisco: Ignatius Press, 1985), 156.

5. See, for example John 3:16 and 1 John 4:7-8.

6. Mark 3:17.

7. The Roman Ritual, translation by the author.

8. Maria Augusta Trapp, *Around the Year with the Trapp Family* (New York: Pantheon, 1955), 64–65.

9. Augustine of Hippo, Sermon 10 on the Saints.

10. Francis X. Weiser, *Handbook of Christian Feasts and Customs* (New York: Harcourt, Brace, & World, 1958), 133.

11. Joanna Bogle, *A Book of Feasts and Seasons* (Leominster, UK: Gracewing, 1992), 59.

12. Weiser, *Handbook*, 133.

13. Clement A. Miles, *Christmas in Ritual and Tradition, Christian and Pagan* (London: T. Fisher Unwin, 1912), 315.

14. See Weiser, *Handbook*, 133–34.

15. Francis X. Weiser, *Religious Customs in the Family: The Radiation of the Liturgy into Christian Homes* (Collegeville, Minnesota: Liturgical Press, 1956), 62.

16. Katherine Burton and Helmut Ripperger, *Feast Day Cookbook* (Catholic Authors Press, 1951 and 2005), 170.

17. Weiser, *Handbook*, 139.

18. *Enchiridion of Indulgences*, 60.

19. Miles, *Christmas in Ritual*, 326.

20. Maurice Lindsay, "Auld Lang Syne," *The Burns Encyclopedia*, 3rd ed. (1996), http://www.robertburns.org/encyclopedia/AuldLangSyne.5.shtml.

21. In some places, this feast was held on January 14 to commemorate the Flight into Egypt.

22. Miles, *Christmas in Ritual*, 322.

23. Ibid., 323.

24. Ibid., 321–22.

25. Weiser, *Handbook*, 152–53.

26. For these and other Twelfth Night customs, see Weiser, *Handbook*, 126–28.

CHAPTER THIRTEEN: KEEP GOING

1. Gerry Bowler, *The World Encyclopedia of Christmas* (Toronto: McClelland & Stewart Ltd., 2000), 128.

2. Robert Herrick, "Ceremony upon Candlemas Eve," Luminarium, http://www.luminarium.org/sevenlit/herrick/candlemas.htm.

3. Francis X. Weiser, *Handbook of Christian Feasts and Customs* (New York: Harcourt, 1958), 152–53.

4.   See Exodus 13:2, 12–13; Numbers 18:15–16.

5.   Weiser, *Handbook*, 299–300.

INDEX